WHAT BECAME OF WYSTAN

What Became of Wystan

CHANGE AND CONTINUITY
IN AUDEN'S POETRY

• • •

ALAN JACOBS

THE UNIVERSITY OF ARKANSAS PRESS
FAYETTEVILLE
1998

03   02   01   00   99   5   4   3   2   1

First paperback printing 1999

Designed by Alice Gail Carter

⊗   The paper used in this publication meets the minimum
requirements of the American National Standard for Permanence of Paper for Printed Library Materials   Z39.48-1984.

Library of Congress Cataloging-in-Publication Data

Jacobs, Alan, 1958–
    What became of Wystan : change and continuity in
    Auden's poetry / Alan Jacobs.
        p.   cm.
    Includes bibliographical references and index.
    ISBN 1-55728-503-9 (cloth : alk. paper)
    ISBN 1-55728-582-9 (paper : alk. paper)
    1. Auden, W. H. (Wystan Hugh), 1907–1973—Criticism
and interpretation. 2. Homosexuality and literature—
United States—History—20th century. 3. Christianity
and literature—United States—History—20th century.
4. English poetry—American influences.   I. Title
PR6001.U4Z752   1998
811'.52—dc21   98-11932
                                                    CIP

for John Burke

Among other things, what became clear to me was that one should watch out when Auden makes his witty comments and observations, keeping an eye on civilization no matter what his immediate subject (or condition) is. I felt that I was dealing with a new kind of metaphysical poet, a man of terrific lyrical gifts, who disguised himself as an observer of public mores. And my suspicion was that this choice of mask, the choice of this idiom, had less to do with matters of style and tradition than with the personal humility imposed on him not so much by a particular creed as by his sense of the nature of language. Humility is never chosen.

• • •

Whatever the reasons for which he crossed the Atlantic and became American, the result was that he fused both idioms of English and became—to paraphrase one of his own lines—a transatlantic Horace. One way or another, all the journeys he took—through lands, caves of the psyche, doctrines, creeds—served not so much to improve his argument as to expand his diction. If poetry ever was for him a matter of ambition, he lived long enough for it to become simply a means of existence. Hence his autonomy, sanity, equipoise, irony, detachment—in short, wisdom.

—JOSEPH BRODSKY

Acknowledgments

Many people have helped me make this book, some of them in ways that they aren't even aware of. My thanks go first to Daniel Albright, who introduced me to serious reflection on Auden's work and for whom, years ago, I first wrote about Auden. Among those who have encouraged, supported, and, when necessary, prodded me in the last three or so years, I wish especially to thank the late Donald Davie, Dana Gioia, David Jeffrey, Charles Marsh, and Mark Noll. My dear friends and colleagues in the English department at Wheaton College, Gail Kienitz and Roger Lundin, have been working on me for much longer and have been truly constant in their support. I am particularly grateful to Donald Marshall for his careful and responsive reading of the whole manuscript and also for his warm encouragement. The editors of the University of Arkansas Press, and the anonymous readers of the manuscript, have provided much valuable advice.

Anyone who chooses to write about Auden these days owes an almost incalculable debt to Auden's literary executor, editor, and best critic, Edward Mendelson. But I must thank him also for his willingness to respond to the repeated bombardments of e-mail I have inflicted on him since I began this project. He has saved me from error more than a few times and would undoubtedly have saved me still more often had I carried out the scheme I once considered of e-mailing him the entire manuscript.

This book would have taken at least another year to write had it not been for the help of Angie Aubrey, Genelle Gertz, Jeanene Skillen, Dora Ton, and especially Phil Burroughs.

This book would very likely have gone unwritten altogether were it not for the generosity of the Evangelical Scholarship Initiative of the Pew Charitable Trusts. I am very grateful for their investment of faith, and money, in my work. The Aldeen Fund at Wheaton College also provided vital financial assistance at several points in my journey. A Summer Study Grant from the National Endowment for the Humanities, though it was not at first directly related to this project, enabled me to learn a great deal I needed to know in order to write about Auden.

I am indebted to the competence and patience of the staff of the Berg Collection at the New York Public Library. At the Bodleian Library of Oxford University, Judith Priestman and Bodley's Librarian, David Vaisey, were not only helpful but graciously so. My thanks also to Donald Sniegowski for introducing me to Mr. Vaisey.

If it is difficult to thank one's friends properly, formulating the proper terms of gratitude for one's family seems well-nigh impossible. My wife Teri, constant in all things, has been constant in her support and love. Since my son Wesley was not yet born when I began writing this book, he is perhaps less aware of his contribution; but the refreshment of spirit he brings to me each day is a gift whose value would be hard to overestimate.

Finally: if I know anything at all about what it means to study literature faithfully and with care, that is largely due to the man to whom I have dedicated this book.

Parts of this book have appeared, in different form, in the *American Scholar* (portions of chapters 5 and 6), *English Language Notes* (the appendix), *The Hudson Review* (chapter 4), and *Religion and Literature* (chapter 2). My thanks to them for their permission to use that work in this context.

For permission to quote from Auden's letter of May 5, 1963, to Monroe Spears, I am indebted to the Estate of W. H. Auden and to the Berg Collection of English and American Literature at the New York Public Library (Astor, Lenox and Tilden Foundations).

Contents

Abbreviations

Full bibliographical information on these works by Auden may be found in the list of works cited.

CP   *Collected Poems* (1991)

DH   *The Dyer's Hand*

EA   *The English Auden*

F&A   *Forewords and Afterwords*

L   *W. H. Auden and Chester Kallman: Libretti and Other Dramatic Writings by W. H. Auden, 1939–1973* (*The Complete Works of W. H. Auden*, Volume II)

SP   *Selected Poems* (1979)

Introduction

In 1960 Philip Larkin wrote for the *Spectator* a review of what was then Auden's newest collection of poems, *Homage to Clio*. The review appeared under the title "What's Become of Wystan?" It encapsulates quite neatly, as perhaps only Randall Jarrell's critiques could do as well, the prevailing view of the later Auden among those who had admired his early poetry.[1] Three assertions characterize Larkin's appraisal of Auden. First, that "after 1940" (the year that Auden returned to the Christian faith of his childhood, and the year after his move to America) Auden became a wholly different poet than he had been: he "elected to remake his entire poetic equipment" (126). Second, that the remade Auden was almost indescribably inferior to his previous incarnation: "too verbose to be memorable and too intellectual to be moving" (123). And third, that by remaking himself Auden had betrayed his admirers collectively, a conviction evident in Larkin's tendency to use plural pronouns to express his censure, as though to emphasize that it was not he as an individual who had been disappointed but rather he as representative of a great mass: "The appearance of his latest collection . . . marks the end of the third decade of Auden's poetic life and does not alter the fact that almost all we value is still confined to its first ten years" (123). "In the end that is what our discontent comes down to: Auden no longer touches our imaginations" (128).

That third assertion is the only one of the three which I will not consider at length in this book, because it is the one which I find to be most obviously correct: Auden had indeed ceased to touch the imaginations of the "great mass" of British literary intellectuals. One might contend that Auden enforced this "discontent." It is obvious that as his stature grew throughout the thirties, his discomfort grew along with it; and, since the word "Audenesque" came into the language as early as 1933, when the poet was twenty-six years old, and the phrase "the Auden age" was in use by the time he turned thirty (Cunningham 18, 20), it may not be too gross an abuse of simile to say that, just as Jesus crossed the Sea of Galilee to escape the multitudes, so Auden crossed the Atlantic to escape his fans.[2] He thereby hoped to avoid suffering as a young and living man what, from the safe refuge of New York City, he would claim had happened to Yeats after his death: "he became his admirers" (CP 197). Clearly, the move to America, and even the conversion to Christianity, represented for Auden means of distancing himself from the expectations British intellectual culture had for him—clearing imaginative space for himself, as Harold Bloom might say, though in this case the threat comes not from distinguished predecessors but from impatient followers seeking signs and wonders. Moreover, as François Duchêne has argued, Auden recognized that his early work "lacked the sense of firm design pointing towards inner necessity," and this recognition, with its accompanying desire to achieve truly great work, also contributed to his willed dislocation (126).[3]

Still, it is not clear that Auden changed as dramatically as Larkin and others thought or that he changed in the way that they thought. Auden himself claimed not to believe that his work had changed dramatically: in 1963 he told Monroe Spears, whose book on him he had just seen in proof, "I am particularly pleased that you seem to perceive, what I hoped was there, a continuity and development of an outlook on the world, not a succession of unrelated ideologies" (Berg Collection). Auden's opinion on this subject is hardly definitive—his memory tended to smooth out ambiguities and ambivalences in his earlier life and work—but it is worth considering. Much of this book will be devoting to considering it.

It is true, however, that Auden could speak in rather different terms. For instance, in an essay written just a few years before his comment to Spears, he told a story about a poetic career. Of the middle-aged poet (who, though referred to always in the third person, is clearly an autobiographical figure) he writes, "Having spent twenty years learning to be himself, he finds that he must now start learning not to be himself. . . . Discovering oneself is a passive process because the self is already there. Time and attention are all it takes. But changing oneself means changing in one direction rather than another, and towards one goal rather than another. The goal may be unknown but movement is impossible without a hypothesis as to where it lies" (DH 52). But however different the vocabulary, this statement scarcely contradicts what Auden said to Spears and is properly read as an expanded treatment of the same theme. That this is so becomes evident when one reads another characteristically Audenesque example of displaced autobiography, a comment he made in an essay on Stravinsky:

> The minor artist . . . once he has reached maturity and found himself, ceases to have a history. A major artist, on the other hand, is always refinding himself, so that the history of his works recapitulates or mirrors the history of art. Once he has done something to his satisfaction, he forgets it and attempts to do something new which he has never attempted before. It is only when he is dead that we are able to see that his various creations, taken together, form one consistent *oeuvre*. Moreover, it is only in the light of his later works that we are able properly to understand his earlier.   (F&A 434)

What seems to be at work here is Auden's admission that his work gives every appearance of dramatic change, and his attempt to make the counter-argument that such change is relatively superficial, the product of a mind continually striving to understand itself and formulate its proper direction. Only a properly and carefully historical reading of the development of his poetry will reveal that the changes do not indicate a mere "succession of unrelated ideologies" but rather ever-closer approximations of an ideal that is itself coming into view only gradually.[4] In general, as Stan Smith has pointed out in a brief lucid survey of what Auden's critics have said on this issue, admirers of the later Auden (mostly American, and mostly Christian in one way or another) tend to share the poet's view on this point, while admirers of the early Auden tend to focus on discontinuity and rupture. (Smith himself is in the latter group, though he claims to join it not because he thinks Auden a turncoat but because he thinks the notion of a unified self an ideologically driven fiction [11]. This is a point to which we will return in chapter 1.)

The question I wish to explore is, then, in its simplest form, What became of Wystan? How did he change after he came to America, and how much did he change? This will not be in any sense a survey of his later work; indeed, some of the most important poems of his later career will be ignored here. (There are surveys aplenty of Auden's work; surveys tend to be the rule in Auden criticism, Lucy McDiarmid's *Auden's Apologies for Poetry* being a notable and welcome exception.) Instead, I have tried to focus my attention on poems which represent transitional moments in Auden's thinking—moments at which some kind of shift seems to be taking place. Most of these moments come during Auden's first few years in America, the war years, in large part, because Auden was working so hard to think through his intellectual situation that he became, for the only time in his life, truly and even astonishingly prolific. In addition to the hundreds of reviews and essays he wrote from 1939 to '45 and dramatic works like *Paul Bunyan*, the poetry he wrote during those six years takes up well over a third of the pages in his *Collected Poems*. All this while he was also teaching at the University of Michigan, Swarthmore, and other American colleges and universities. If, as Auden claimed, he developed slowly, that development must have been accelerated by the wild pace of his writing in those tumultuous years.

Something of what became of Wystan may perhaps be captured in a geological metaphor: certain poems represent fault lines, points at which massive tectonic plates meet, but it is not always easy to tell how great the tension is at the point of contact. As they grind against each other there will always be slippage; in some cases minor adjustments only will be required to relieve the pressure, but in others a more dramatic and dangerous concussion may eventuate. What the interested observer must do, then, is to survey not only the fault lines themselves, but also the surrounding territory.

For instance, Auden's thinking about love and sex changed, quite dramatically, as a result of his meeting Chester Kallman and returning to Christianity (two events that occurred within little more than a year): he began almost at the same time to think of himself as a married person and to reflect on agape, or divine love; both considerations marked a considerable change from his earlier views. The relevant fault line in this particular case may be examined in the poem "In Sickness and in Health" (1940), but this poem can be fully understood only in relation to thematically similar poems from points earlier and later in Auden's career (chiefly, "Lay your sleeping head, my love" [1937] and "In Praise of Limestone" [1948]). An exploration of these matters is the burden of my fifth chapter.

The "tectonic plates" which produce such "fault lines" are traditions —chiefly what the philosopher Alasdair MacIntyre calls "traditions of moral inquiry." MacIntyre's use of the word *tradition* is somewhat less familiar to literary scholars than that of T. S. Eliot, or Hans-Georg Gadamer, from both of which it differs in important ways. For both Eliot and Gadamer, the word *tradition* is likely to appear, if not literally at least by implication, with a capital T; it is also rarely deployed in the plural, or preceded by an article. Tradition for these writers—though in other respects they do not mean the same thing by it—is something unitary and essential. "Tradition," says Eliot, famously, "cannot be inherited, and if you want it you must obtain it by great labour" (*Selected* 5)—or, to paraphrase, work out your own tradition with fear and trembling. "The real force of morals," says Gadamer, "is based on tradition. . . . This is precisely what we call tradition: the ground of their validity" (280–81).

MacIntyre, on the other hand, is interested in what it means to live in a society characterized by the presence of multiple traditions, in the forms taken by the conflicts among those traditions, and in the possibilities of adjudicating those conflicts. Moreover, MacIntyre places a particular emphasis on the dialectical nature of each tradition when properly understood, even from within and by its proponents. "A tradition is an argument extended through time," writes MacIntyre in his most comprehensive exploration of these questions (*Whose* 12); and in a brief essay which encapsulates the chief concerns of his recent books, he claims that

To belong to a tradition is to be engaged in an essentially communal form of rational existence in which persons so engaged offer commentary upon the achievements of their predecessors and upon the limitations of those achievements, commentary which is then subjected to the objections, elaborations, and emendations of others at work in the same tradition.   ("Traditions" 10)

In his first years in America, Auden experienced a growing conviction that the left-liberalism for which he had become, however unwillingly, a spokesman was, though it claimed to transcend and repudiate traditions, itself a tradition and therefore subject to evaluation in relation to other, competing traditions. Auden also thought this way quite consciously, and therefore does not just fit neatly within MacIntyre's conceptual framework, but rather is in a significant sense MacIntyre's predecessor in considering the conflicts among and within traditions. It is true that early in Auden's time in America he could sound the jeremiad note almost as well as the Christian Eliot—for example, in 1941 he wrote, "The machine has destroyed tradition in the old sense and the refusal to replace it by absolute presuppositions deliberately chosen and consciously held is leading us to disaster" ("Criticism" 141)—but as his reading in history and theology and his consideration of their lessons grew deeper, he sounded less like a person preparing to repel the barbarians at the gate than like a person who understood that, even after one chooses a tradition, one's understanding of that tradition is subject to continual renegotiation.

I hope that the remainder of this book will bear out these contentions. The first chapter considers in a general way the question, much neglected in literary study, of change—personal as opposed to institutional change. (About the latter literary theorists have had much to say.) Chapter 2 is concerned with the dominant poetic tradition that Auden rejected (Romanticism), and chapter 3 with a neglected one he reclaimed (Horatianism). In the thirties Auden was much occupied by an attempt to synthesize the Marxian and Freudian vocabularies; this attempt, and these vocabularies, he virtually abandoned soon after he arrived in America; and therefore chapters 4 and 5 explore changes in his thinking about, respectively, political and psycho-sexual matters.

The last chapter turns the tables, as it were, and pursues what appears to be a notable continuity in Auden's work almost from beginning to end: his preference for mixed literary forms, and specifically that mongrel genre known to Mikhail Bakhtin as the menippea and to Northrop Frye as the anatomy. But if the preference is continuous, the reasons for it may not be. Genres are themselves small traditions, but of an ideologically malleable kind: they may be used in remarkably varied ways by more comprehensive traditions, which are always voracious consumers of rhetorical resources. I describe this last chapter at greater length in order to reinforce what is perhaps the guiding principle of this study, that neither change nor continuity are always what they seem.

WHAT BECAME OF WYSTAN

CHAPTER 1

Change

Though all our ideas true or false are the product of our experience, i.e., of our way of living, it is legitimate to see ideas as the prime agents of human historical change, for were it not for his capacity to think, man's evolution would be complete like that of the animals. An idea has two purposes, to justify our satisfactions, and to find a way to remove our wants. In its aspect as justification, an idea is a pure reflection of our material life and neither can re-enter history as an effective agent nor wants to. In its aspect as a means to remove wants, it demands a change in our actions and so becomes an agent of change.
— THE PROLIFIC AND THE DEVOURER

What do we mean when we say, "She changed her mind"? How can a mind be changed? And who is the "she" who does the changing, if (as the structure of the sentence implies) this "she" is somehow separate from, or encompasses, the "mind" that is changed? Moreover, why do we use this phrase chiefly when discussing relatively insignificant alterations in thinking—"At first I wanted the chocolate one, but then I changed my mind"—rather than for the truly major transformations which the language would seem to imply? After all, it would seem odd to hear someone say, "I used to worship Satan, but then I changed my mind" or even, "I used to be a Marxist, but then I changed my mind." No, in common usage "changing one's mind" seems to refer largely to minor and causally vague adjustments of intellectual position, not conversions, transformations, or serious reconsiderations of one's thought.

It is "changing one's mind" in this uncommonly strong sense with which this book will be occupied. How and why, at the end of the 1930s and the beginning of the 1940s, did W. H. Auden change his mind? During this period he ended his long and ambivalent flirtation with Marxism, repudiated (though not in every detail) the Freudian image of the self, and reclaimed the Christian faith of his childhood. What forces brought about these profound redirections?

It is not the kind of topic with which literary scholars today appear comfortable. Among the theoretical concepts and categories which seek to describe or explain change, we prefer those which operate on the level of institutions, disciplines, or interpretive communities rather than persons. We tend to talk as though we were social constructionists, that is, as though we believed that all personal beliefs and commitments are determined by the culture into which the person is born, even though most of us are not social constructionists. We simply lack an acceptable vocabulary, or a vocabulary we feel to be acceptable, for talking in any other way. What Thomas Kuhn and Michel Foucault have done for the terminology of institutional change remains to be done for those of us who retain an interest in how persons change.

This situation has a curious history. As Charles Taylor has shown in his great book *Sources of the Self*, modernism repudiates certain features of the Romantic-expressivist understanding of selfhood, but nevertheless remains within the tradition of selfhood which finds its "sources" in Augustine, Luther, Montaigne, Descartes—the usual suspects, and properly so (see especially chapters 23–25). Existentialism may have been anti-Romantic in some ways, but in others it was merely a continuation of the old project of selfhood. If we are indeed in a post-modern era, and not merely continuing the work of modernism (as

Jürgen Habermas most forcefully has argued, especially in *Theory of Communicative Action* and *The Philosophical Discourse of Modernity*), that "new era" is marked most clearly by various attempts to repudiate the project of selfhood—most such attempts being weak or strong versions of social constructionism.

Even those of us who are not social constructionists are profoundly influenced by their claims and are reluctant to speak too readily in terms which smell of an earlier time. This makes it difficult for us to respond to writers like Auden except in a confrontational way, for though his was a chastened understanding of selfhood, the notion of the cultivation of the self was absolutely central to his thinking. After being wildly enthusiastic about Kierkegaard for a few years, Auden came to believe that Kierkegaard simply failed to comprehend the *material* constraints upon the self: "A planetary visitor might read through the whole of his voluminous works without discovering that human beings are not ghosts but have bodies of flesh and blood" (*Modern* 42). A bit closer to Auden's own view would be that of Reinhold Niebuhr, from a book which Auden liked to assign in the university classes he taught:

> To a certain degree man is free to reject one environment for another. If he dislikes the spiritual environment of the twentieth century he may consciously choose to live by the patterns of the thirteenth century. If he finds his physical environment uncongenial he has the capacity to modify it. The pride of modern man has sometimes tempted him to forget that there are limits of creatureliness which he cannot transcend and that there are inexorable forces of nature which he cannot defy. It is nevertheless important to remember that human spirituality is sharply distinguished from animal existence by the measure of human freedom and the consequent degree of discrete and unique individuality in man.   (*Nature* 56)

Though Niebuhr is at some pains here to emphasize what Richard Rorty would call "contingency"—a contingency which for Niebuhr derives not from socialization but from our status as "creatures," as beings made by an almighty God—the overall tone of the passage jangles in the postmodern ear. The repeated use of the word "man" troubles us not only by its sexism, but also because we know Foucault's argument (in both *The Order of Things* and *Discipline and Punish*) about the emergence of the concept of "man" as the distinctive invention of modernity. And the idea that a twentieth-century person can in any meaningful sense "choose" the world of the thirteenth century seems to us self-evidently absurd.

Nevertheless, unless we do embrace a strict social constructionism, the vocabulary of selfhood and choice need not be utterly abandoned; there may be some virtue in taking such notions seriously, without aggressively contesting them—especially since they allow us to discuss the question of how people do change, a question which social constructionism has had considerable difficulty dealing with. It may be that the mature Auden's view of selfhood—which, as I hope to show, is more constrained and hence more tenable to us than Niebuhr's— has certain descriptive powers which we would be unwise to neglect until we have something better.

In an essay called simply "Change," Stanley Fish takes a stab at the problem. He begins by describing

> a student in a graduate seminar in literary theory who acknowledged that in the course of the semester he had been persuaded to the conventionalist views I have been describing. What bothered him was the very fact that he had been persuaded, for, given those same views, he didn't see how his mind could have been changed. He had, after all, been a member of an interpretive community, and indeed of a *literary* interpretive community, when he entered my class. How is it that he was able to move out of that community and into another?   (*Doing* 145)

Fish's answer, in brief, is that the question of how a mind changes is an incoherent question because "the mind (and, by extension, the community) is an engine of change, an ongoing project whose operations are at once constrained and the means by which those same constraints can be altered" (146). The parenthetical phrase here is the key one because Fish is really interested only in the community, scarcely at all in the mind. He never mentions the student again, even when some of his statements could address quite directly the student's concern. For instance, the student believed that he had left one inter-pretive community and entered another, when according to Fish's scheme it would be more accurate to say that he had merely revised his understanding of the community within which he remained: "an interpretive community . . . is at once homogeneous with respect to some general sense of purpose or purview, and heterogeneous with respect to the variety of practices it can accommodate" (149). But this point appears in the context of Fish's explanation of the relations between literary criticism and linguistics; in other words, it is a point about institutions and communities, not persons or minds. To the student who wanted to know how his mind was changed, the essence of Fish's reply is that his mind doesn't exist: instead of a mind he has what some theorists like to call a "site of ideological contestation," a field where various forces meet and interact, a field whose character (if such a word applies) is always being modified by the incessantly shifting patterns of those forces.[1]

It seems to me that these notions are more obviously applicable to institutions than to (what we call) minds. This is not to say that Fish's deconstruction of the concept of mind is necessarily wrong, only that it is not evidently right, and can scarcely be asserted as blithely as he asserts it. His equation of the way minds work with the way commu-nities work is equally problematic. Those of us who find Fish's evolv-ing explanations of institutional change intriguing or even compelling may wish for a more substantial theory of, to use the conventional language which Fish dislikes, how minds change.

For Fish the collapse of foundationalism, and more generally of Enlightenment canons of rationality, eradicates the old distinctions between changes made on the basis of principle and those made on the basis of mere preference, between rationally justifiable changes or beliefs and arbitrary, unjustifiable changes or beliefs. Fish replaces these lost distinctions with the conceptual apparatus of the pragmatist tradi-tion, at least as it has been identified and celebrated by Richard Rorty.[2] But not all thinkers see pragmatism as the inevitable alternative to foundationalism: Alasdair MacIntyre, in particular, has attempted to formulate and defend a conception of rationality that does not rely on the canons of the Enlightenment, but instead recognizes that all beliefs derive from one's adherence (conscious or unconscious) to certain traditions of inquiry: we believe what we believe not through the exercise of pure and unmediated rationality but through our having been educated in certain traditions. Nevertheless, in MacIntyre's view, some traditions are superior to others, more rational than others; they just have to demonstrate their rationality, not through an appeal to some "self-sufficient, self-justifying epistemological first principles," but through their own dialectical history, which includes their relations to other traditions (*Whose* 360). What MacIntyre calls a "tradition of inquiry" resembles what Fish calls an "interpretive community," so their initial descriptions of the problem faced by Fish's student do not seriously differ. But MacIntyre is more willing than Fish to explore what happens when a person is faced with either a conflict between rival traditions or conflicting understandings of the nature of a single tradition.[3]

First of all, MacIntyre insists—and here Fish would wholly agree—that there can never be a valid universal account of change. When faced with the claims of various traditions of inquiry into, say, the nature of interpretation or the potential existence of God, a person is faced, says MacIntyre, with a question: What would be a rational response to these conflicting claims?

> The initial answer is: that will depend on who you are and how you understand yourself. . . . [T]he problems of . . . how to confront the rival claims of traditions contending with each other in the *agon* of ideological encounter are not one and the same set of problems for all persons. What those problems are, how they are to be formulated and addressed, and how, if at all, they may be resolved will vary not only with the historical, social, and cultural situation of the persons whose problems these are but also with the history of belief and attitude of each particular person up to the point at which he or she finds these problems inescapable.   (*Whose* 393)

Having made this clarification, MacIntyre goes on to suggest that, in the contemporary world, there are three common types of response to the conflict of traditions.

"There is first of all that of the type of person for whom what an encounter with some particular tradition . . . may provide is an occasion for self-recognition and self-knowledge. . . . Upon encountering a coherent presentation of one particular tradition of rational enquiry, either in its seminal texts or in some later, perhaps contemporary, restatement of its positions, such a person will often experience a shock of recognition: *this* is not only, so such a person may say, what I now take to be true but in some measure what I have always taken to be true" (394). Accounts of European intellectuals' responses to communism, especially in the early years of this century, are filled with descriptions of experiences of just this kind. Ignazio Silone is perhaps the best example of what Arthur Koestler once called a "natural communist," one whose commitments to radical political change were formed long before he ever read a word of Marx (quoted by Walzer 101). But it is important to note, in the context of Auden's conversion, that until recently it was virtually impossible for any European or American intellectual to have such an experience regarding Christianity, since its doctrines and stories were so deeply imbedded in the culture and would become familiar to any child in the process of acquiring cultural literacy. (Incidentally, Auden's biographer Humphrey Carpenter describes Auden's adherence to Marxism as something that came about gradually [147–53]; the same may be said for his disillusionment with it.)

MacIntyre's second type of response comes from "the person who finds him or herself an alien to every tradition of enquiry which he or she encounters and who does so because he or she brings to the encounter with such traditions standards of rational justification which the beliefs of no tradition could satisfy."

To MacIntyre, "This is the kind of post-Enlightenment person who responds to the failure of the Enlightenment to provide neutral, impersonal tradition-independent standards of rational judgment by concluding that no set of beliefs proposed for acceptance is therefore justifiable. The everyday world is to be treated as one of pragmatic necessities. Every scheme of overall belief which extends beyond the realm of pragmatic necessity is equally unjustified" (395). It is not clear whether MacIntyre accepts Rorty's account of this tradition, with its

roots in Nietzsche as fully as in James and Dewey; it is clear that pragmatism was not understood in this sense in Auden's time, and moreover that none of these figures had major significance for Auden.
(Though, according to Alan Ansen, Auden once made a wonderfully
curious indirect remark about Dewey while discussing what he wanted
to put into the anthology that became *The Portable Greek Reader*:
"Isocrates reminds me of John Dewey. He's a mediocrity who's usually
right whereas Plato is a man of genius who's always wrong" [74–75].)

MacIntyre then presents a kind of tertium quid: "Most of our contemporaries do not live at or even near that point of extremity [exem-
plified by person 2], but neither are they for the most part able to
recognize in themselves in their encounters with traditions that they
have already implicitly to some significant degree given their allegiance
to some one particular tradition. Instead they tend to live betwixt and
between, accepting usually unquestioningly the assumptions of the
dominant liberal individualist forms of public life, but drawing in
different areas of their lives upon a variety of tradition-generated
resources of thought and action, transmitted from a variety of familial,
religious, educational, and other social and cultural sources" (397).

It seems clear that Auden belonged to this third category. The key
difference, however, between Auden and a typical member of this
camp is that Auden was not content to be a mere *bricoleur*, drawing
whenever possible or necessary from whatever tradition of inquiry
was handy, but constantly sought to organize and combine various
traditions into an intellectual equivalent of a unified field theory.
Auden was an inveterate maker of charts and for more than a decade
preceding his conversion occasionally worked on identifying and
codifying the potential links among Christianity, Marxism, and
psychoanalysis. In a notebook he used while living in Berlin in 1929,
he put together a "Glossary of Christian and Psychological terms"
which apparently was intended to show, if not the compatibility, at
least the structural similarity between the two systems—almost as if
he were groping toward a Jungian-archetypal syncretism. Here are the
first few entries (quoted by Mendelson, *Early* 76):

Heaven	The Unconscious
Earth	The Conscious Mind
Hell	The repressed unconscious
Purgatory	The consulting-room

The Father {Body?}	The Ego-instincts	the self ideal
The Son {Mind?}	The Death-instincts	the not-Self ideal
The Holy Ghost	The Libido	The relation between these two opposites

When, a few years later, Auden sought to escape the isolation imposed upon the artist by Romantic and modernist aesthetics, and to discover a viable social role for the poet, he returned to this chart and added (to the left of the Christian column) Marxist equivalents: the "Collective" for the "Father," the "Individual" for the "Son," "History" for the "Holy Ghost," and so on (145–46). Similarly, in his 1935 essay "Psychology and Art To-day" he produces another chart that recasts the relations between Christianity and psychoanalysis in chronological terms, dividing Western history since the advent of Christianity into three periods that show a broad cultural movement toward the psychoanalytic understanding of human identity and, almost as a footnote at the bottom of the chart, toward socialism as the reigning political structure (EA 338).

Auden's last great foray into such deliberate syncretism before his conversion to Christianity comes in 1939, in the later-abandoned collection of aphorisms and mini-essays ("my pensées," he called them in a letter [Bucknell and Jenkins, In Solitude 108]) entitled The Prolific and the Devourer. Here he evidently has come to believe that politics and psychology must be subsumed under some form of religious commitment. The religion that he articulates does not involve a belief in gods or a god, or in the supernatural, or in life after death. Auden explicitly disavows all of these beliefs (81–83). What, then, is the content of this religion? First of all it reveres Jesus, not as the Son of God, but as the most penetrating analyst of the human condition and the most gifted of all prophets who would enjoin us to pursue virtue and goodness. Indeed, it is just this pursuit which forms the core of the religion that Auden attempts to articulate in The Prolific and the

Devourer. It is properly called a religion because the demands it places upon us are more binding and universally significant than those of mere morality; for instance, "I believe that our experience forces us to think the nature of the laws which govern the relations of forms is one which when described in terms of relations between conscious human beings we call Love" (82). But again, it differs from what is usually called religion by its utter unconcern for questions about the existence of God: "If anyone chooses to call our knowledge of existence knowledge of God, to call Essence the Father, Form the Son, and Motion the Holy Ghost, I don't mind: Nomenclature is purely a matter of convenience." In this and in several other respects the position Auden is working through in *The Prolific* bears a striking resemblance to the moral philosophy of Iris Murdoch, which articulates with considerably more rigor and sophistication the belief that the proper object of worship and devotion is the Good, regardless of the form in which it appears to the worshipper: "Good represents the reality of which God is the dream" (*Metaphysics* 496).

What is most important about *The Prolific* for the purposes of this discussion is that it marks the abandonment of a decade of attempts to think in a certain way about politics, psychology, and religion, whether in chart form or after the manner of the *bricoleur*, that is to say, it marks the recognition that the juxtaposition of various traditions, each considered appropriate and useful within certain spheres of human concern but useless outside those spheres, does not amount to a coherent account of how to live. What is required, Auden is deciding at the time of *The Prolific*, is a master discourse, or as MacIntyre might say, a tradition which is capable of controlling, ordering, and deciding the validity of other traditions, rather than subsisting alongside of them and taking its occasional turns at the helm, according to the demands of a given situation.

But perhaps the term "tradition" is misplaced here. For it is no accident that the title of Auden's work comes from Blake, since he is still operating under the assumption that the formulation of this master discourse is something that he must do on his own: "I must Create a System, or be enslaved by another Man's" (*Jerusalem*, plate 20, line 20).

Yet he also, as we have noted, referred to the book as his "pensées" and had been reading Pascal with considerable attention as he started work on the book—not to mention writing a reflective and admiring poem about Pascal's famous dramatic encounter (as described in his "Memorial") with "Dieu d'Abraham, Dieu d'Isaac, Dieu de Jacob, non des philosophes et savants" (309). And Pascal's task was the defense of an inherited tradition, not the formulation of his own system— indeed, in Auden's poem that tradition commands, or simply *takes*, his assent and his devotion (EA 452–53).[4] Thus Auden's eventual abandonment of *The Prolific* may well indicate his coming to understand that no one can serve two masters, nor two diametrically opposed conceptions of what it means to achieve a coherent philosophy. Within a year of his work on his "pensées," Auden would renounce the attempt to create his own system and accept the authority of the Christian tradition to which Pascal before him had given (or been granted) assent. From this point on, Auden was obliged to consider Marxism and psychoanalysis, indeed all such comprehensive and ambitious systems of explanation, chiefly as traditions which rivaled rather than complemented or supplemented the one to which he now gave his allegiance.

The rest of this book, then, will be concerned with reconstructing Auden's delineation, in the years of the Second World War, of the various and conflicting traditions which had shaped his mind—or rather, had left it in shapeless disorder—and his attempts to adjudicate among these traditions, if necessary to choose among them, to understand the place of each in an orderly, unified mental field. As the various tectonic plates pressed more forcefully against one another in Auden's mind, some alteration of their relative positions became necessary, some easing of the tension. Critics of Auden are still debating, and will continue to debate, the seismic resonance of the readjustment.

CHAPTER 2

The Critique of Romanticism

Art cannot make a man want to become good, but it can prevent him from imagining that he already is; it cannot give him faith in God, but it can show him his despair.
—"DIDYMUS" [AUDEN], *COMMONWEAL*,
NOVEMBER 6, 1942

How glad I am," Auden once wrote, "that the silliest remark ever made about poets,'the unacknowledged legislators of the world,' was made by a poet whose work I detest" ("Squares" 177). For Auden, Shelley is exemplary of Romanticism's most egregious religio-political pretensions—pretensions which from an early age he found distasteful, but which he attacked with increasing virulence and frequency after his reconversion to Christianity in 1940.[1] Though

Shelley comes in for particular abuse—as he has from so many poets and critics since the advent of modernism—it is Romanticism in general which is Auden's real enemy; and while Homer may be noted for his charity to the Trojans, Auden does not exemplify the same virtue toward the Romantics. Indeed, how could he be expected to do so? For Auden, like so many modernists, was forced to work out his relationship to his great poetic predecessors with fear and trembling. In such a struggle, we should not look for fairness.

Nevertheless, even in time of intellectual war Auden demonstrates a sensitivity and interpretive acuity rarely evident in other modernists' attacks upon their Romantic ancestors. For Auden, Romanticism is not a monolithic entity, but rather a complex and often self-contradictory cultural phenomenon which draws nourishment from diverse sources.[2] Furthermore, it is not a movement confined to the greats of the past and the mediocrities of the present; instead, it is a living force which shapes and directs the careers of even its most vociferous opponents.

Because Auden belongs to the second generation of poetic modernists, a generation able to read Eliot in its formative years (Auden entered Oxford in 1925), anti-Romanticism is with him almost from the beginning of his career; it is a standard feature of his critical rhetoric throughout the thirties. But after Auden's return to the church, he begins to reconsider his understanding of the Romantic movement. The subsequent revaluation is articulated with force in the poem that he considered his masterpiece, *The Sea and the Mirror*; but the poet would continue to reflect on the categories set by that poem through the remainder of his career.

The Sea and the Mirror—subtitled "A Commentary on *The Tempest*" —reads that play as a psychomachia, an object lesson in the temptations of artistic power.[3] For Auden, one of Prospero's (which is to say, the poet's) most dangerous errors is his failure to understand that Ariel is not his to control; furthermore, when Prospero is self-deceived in this way, Ariel will emerge from their inevitable rivalry victorious because the lyrical beauty which the Romantic aesthetic identifies as true poetic power and authority resides in him, not in Prospero.

Prospero's long monologue near the beginning of the poem drama-
tizes his belated recognition of the way things were all along—

> Are all your tricks a test? If so, I hope you find, next time,
>   Someone in whom you cannot spot the weakness
> Through which you will corrupt him with your charm. Mine you did
>   And me you have. . . .   (CP 407)

—a recognition made possible only by his willingness to abandon the
role of conjuror:

> And now, in my old age, I wake, and this journey really exists,
>   And I have actually to take it, inch by inch,
> Alone and on foot, without a cent in my pocket,
>   Through a universe where time is not foreshortened,
> No animals talk, and there is neither floating nor flying.   (409)

A key Romantic error, then, is to assume that the poet controls language and imagination; the truth, rather, is that language and imagination are the unacknowledged legislators of the poets. But at some
point every poet, because poets are merely human, will be forced to
make that acknowledgment.

This warning is pursued in the longest and most brilliant section of
the poem, "Caliban to the Audience." Let us not fall into Prospero's
error: part of his foolishness, says Auden in an essay that articulates
many of the poem's key ideas, is that he believed that the fleshly
Caliban could be ignored, demeaned, pushed out of sight, and that
Ariel could be privileged instead:

> One must admire Prospero because of his talents and his strength;
> one cannot possibly like him. . . . while we have to admit that Caliban
> is both brutal and corrupt, a "lying slave" who can be prevented from
> doing mischief "by stripes not kindness," we cannot help feeling that
> Prospero is largely responsible for his corruption, and that, in the debate
> between them, Caliban has the best of the argument.   (DH 129)

"Caliban to the Audience" is in large part an extended and pointed
warning that Ariel and Caliban cannot be divided, that they are two
poles of a single human psyche, and that to flee one in favor of the

other is to encourage grave psychic distress—chiefly because it is to elevate a partial principle, a half-entity, into a whole and complete idol. To do so, in Auden's view, is close to psychic suicide.[4] In its religious aspect, this partiality is called Manicheanism: "*The Tempest* seems to me a manichean work, not because it shows the relation of Nature to Spirit as one of conflict and hostility, which in fallen man it is, but because it puts the blame for this upon Nature and makes the Spirit innocent" (DH 130).

Nevertheless, while poets, following their model Prospero, tend to shun Caliban in his aesthetic aspect, in the "real world" he is a more tempting and appealing figure: in fact, he becomes none other than Cupid. Auden's logic here is ingenious: Caliban is the personification of our bestial impulses, and Cupid is a god of the sexual instincts that we share with the beasts. The demon, inverted, is the deity. (Or, in other terms, Prospero's Hobbesian vision of the creature unenlightened by reason and civilization becomes, through an ingenious hermeneutical twist, Rousseau's noble savage.)

Having identified the real Caliban, Auden goes on to show that the cult of erotic love is but one manifestation of the pervasive tendency, especially evident in one strand of Romanticism, to seek the ideal in the real. For him, the root of that tendency, distant though it may seem from eroticism, is nostalgia for an Edenic state where desires are innocent and their satisfaction immediate. Auden's Caliban embroiders a brilliant parody of those who would chase childlike innocence, seeking desperately to retrace their path back to Heaven along the clouds of glory they have trailed:

> "Carry me back, Master, to the cathedral town where the canons run through the water meadows with butterfly nets and the old women keep sweetshops in the cobbled side streets. . . . Give me my passage home, let me see that harbour once again just as it was before I learned the bad words. . . . Look, Uncle, look. They have broken my glasses and I have lost my silver whistle. Pick me up, Uncle, let little Johnny ride away on your massive shoulders to recover his green kingdom. . . ."
> (CP 437–38)

But this apparently innocuous desire, argues Caliban, when fully understood proves to be an insatiable lust for "the ultimately liberal condition"; a lust which, when realized, produces a nightmare state "where the possessive note is utterly silent and all events are tautological repetitions and no decision will ever alter the secular stagnation," where the nostalgic get, not what they *thought* they wanted, but what they *really* wanted, which is to be "the only subject. Who, When, Why, the poor tired little historic questions fall wilting into a hush of utter failure." Their "existence is indeed free at last to choose its own meaning, that is, to plunge headlong into despair and fall through silence fathomless and dry" (438–39). The desire for perfect freedom is in fact a desire for a world which can offer no threat to the fragile but invaluable ego; but a world without threat is, by the same token, a world without meaning, for it is only in relation to other selves that we understand our own. Over this condition of pristine and hence perfectly isolated selfhood Caliban-Cupid, elevated by the foolish to the status of deity, presides as the *genius loci*.

Caliban addresses this warning to only a part, though the larger part, of the audience, "you, assorted, consorted specimens of the general popular type, the major flock who have trotted trustingly hither but found, you reproachfully baah, no grazing" (435). There remains, however, "that other, smaller but doubtless finer group among you, . . . whose *amour propre* prefers to turn for help to my more spiritual colleague" (439)—that is, Ariel. They have fallen upon the thorns of life; they bleed; they harbor no hope for an Edenic past; they want out and up. Of Ariel they beg,

> "translate us, bright Angel, from this hell of inert and ailing matter, growing steadily senile in a time forever immature, to that blessed realm, so far above the twelve impertinent winds and the four unreliable seasons, that Heaven of the Really General Case where, tortured no longer by three dimensions and immune from temporal vertigo, Life turns into Light, absorbed for good into the permanently stationary, completely self-sufficient, absolutely reasonable One." (440)

This is the elementary wish, it should be clear, of the aesthete: to escape by means of the purity of art from the depredations of history —history, that entropic movement that, as the Fool says of Lear, grows senile without ever having reached maturity.

To Auden, this desire to awake, like Stephen Dedalus, from history's nightmare is as delusive as that for the ideal-in-real that characterized the followers of Cupid-Caliban; and, like those other fools, the followers of Ariel do not understand what they are asking for. Caliban identifies the true nature of their request as "the wish for . . . direct unentailed power without *any*, however secretly immanent, obligation to inherit or transmit" (440). If the followers of Cupid sought freedom without consequences, the followers of Ariel seek power without consequences, which in practical terms means to owe nothing to the past (no inheritance) or to the future (no transmission).

The complete realization of this desire proves to be a "nightmare of public solitude," just the reverse of Cupid's condition in that there is no shortage of selves, but instead the subject's utter inability to identify them:

> [O]ther selves undoubtedly exist, but though everyone's pocket is bulging with birth certificates, insurance policies, passports and letters of credit, there is no way of proving whether they are genuine or planted or forged, so that no one knows whether another is his friend disguised as an enemy or his enemy disguised as a friend (there is probably no one whose real name is Brown).   (441)

In fact, you cannot really have a name in this "Heaven of the Really General Case," because a name would mark your particularity and implicate you in a history and in human society: if you have a name, you have parents who named you; there are people who know you and call you by that name; you hold some identifiable place among your fellow citizens.

The attempt to escape from the responsibilities inherent in the limitations of identity and thereby to wield unconditioned power over one's self leads to a surprising result, the discovery that what once appeared to be the crippling force of time is in fact a crippled self.

And that crippled self now fills all being:

> Everything, in short, suggests Mind but, surrounded by an infinite
> extension of the adolescent difficulty, a rising of the subjective and
> subjunctive to ever steeper, stormier heights, the panting frozen expres-
> sive gift has collapsed under the strain of its communicative anxiety,
> and contributes nothing by way of meaning but a series of staccato
> barks or a delirious gush of glossolalia.   (441)

The only way to achieve power without consequence is by means of
a hypertrophied "I," a self which so fills the world that there is nothing
to act upon, no one to speak to. In the "Postscript" to the poem we
hear Ariel speaking to Caliban, asserting his love, but each stanza is
echoed by the Prompter with a wispy "I"; in essence, that is all Ariel
can say—and all those who put themselves wholly in his power can say.

Elsewhere in the poem, Caliban describes in hideous detail the fate
of a hypothetical young poet who gives himself over to Ariel, thinking
to escape "the fury and the mire of human veins" (Yeats, *Collected* 248),
living instead in a Byzantium of lyric art. But, says Auden, that lyric
art, sought as a substitute for being in time, cannot sustain the pressure placed upon it, and collapses "under the strain of its communicative anxiety." In a world without distinct and particular selves,
communication is impossible. All that remains, after the collapse, is
the earthly and earthy self so long neglected and now become that
"deformed and salvage slave" Caliban—to cite Yeats again, the very
personification of "the foul rag-and-bone shop of the heart" (348).

As Caliban details his warnings to those who give themselves over
to him or to Ariel, two of Auden's convictions become increasingly
clear: first, that the victims of both fates share the delusion that it
is possible to exercise full control over their destinies; and second,
that the desire for such self-determination is the characteristic disease
of Romanticism. For Auden, Wordsworth exemplifies the poetics of
Caliban-Cupid, determined by a virtually unlimited confidence in the
capacity of the real, at least the real of a personal or cultural past, to contain and manifest the ideal.[5] The brilliant sarcasm of the imagined pleas

of Cupid's would-be disciples—"'Pick me up, Uncle, let little Johnny ride away on your massive shoulders to recover his green kingdom'"— is largely a parody of the Wordsworthian vision of the innocent past. Similarly, the "infinite extension of the adolescent difficulty, [the] rising of the subjective and the subjunctive to ever steeper, stormier heights" to which Ariel leads *his* poor wretches, represents Auden's more serious and more bitter attack on Shelley's conception of the poet: apparently all-powerful yet in the end utterly superfluous.[6] In each case Auden turns a beatific vision into an infernal one by application of Dante's principle of *contrapasso*, according to which sinners reside eternally with and in the sin they chose during their earthly lives ("Qual io fui vivo, tal son morto," says one of them, with an unconscious irony: "What I was in life I am in death" [*Inferno* XIV:51]).[7]

For the adherents of each myth—the Wordsworthian myth of freedom and the Shelleyan myth of power—the consequences are essentially the same: "Such are the alternative routes, the facile glad-handed highway or the virtuous averted track, by which the human effort to make its own fortune arrives all eager at its abruptly dreadful end" (CP 442). If the first and greatest sin is pride, for Auden the Romantic quest for autonomous selfhood is but a peculiarly modern manifestation of that sin, and the true believers in Romanticism's myths must bear the consequences they, like Dante's damned, have chosen for themselves.[8]

But what alternative to these two infernal paths does Auden envision?[9] He lays down some of the conditions for a viable response in an essay that compares Baudelaire and Tennyson: "Baudelaire was right in seeing that art is beyond good and evil, and Tennyson was a fool to try to write a poetry that would teach the Ideal; but Tennyson was right in seeing that an art which is beyond good and evil is a game of secondary importance, and Baudelaire was a victim of his own pride in persuading himself that a mere game was *'le meilleur témoignage / que nous puissions donner de notre dignité'*" (F&A 231).[10] If art is beyond good and evil, that is not its glory—a "mere game" can confer no dignity. Nevertheless, it is the best we can do. The poet's choice is all too clear: it is Hobson's choice.

And what makes this dilemma dangerous is the possibility that the "game" could intrude upon and even displace the real. In the same essay, Auden claims that "trash is the inevitable result whenever a person tries to do for himself or for others by the writing of poetry what can only be done in some other way, by action, or study, or prayer." Once the poet learns that "*something* can be achieved by artistic creation, namely a consciousness of what one really feels," he may easily succumb to "the temptation to think that everything can be achieved in this way; the elimination, for example, of unpleasant or disgraceful feelings"(F&A 225).[11] The practical consequence of this doctrine is that the poet, if he must deal with matters of ultimate concern, must not attempt to treat them directly and mimetically, but instead must keep a respectful analogical distance.

It would follow that the more distantly analogical poetry is, the less likely it is to fall into the Romantic inferno. And indeed, near the end of his monologue in *The Sea and the Mirror* Caliban worries that his virtuoso mimicry of his audience's hopes and fears might have been altogether *too* good: "I begin to feel something of the serio-comic embarrassment of the dedicated dramatist, who, in representing to you your condition of estrangement from the truth, is doomed to fail the more he succeeds, for the more truthfully he paints the condition, the less clearly can he indicate the truth from which it is estranged. . . ." (CP 442).

With this insight we are finally beginning to see the light at the end of Auden's tunnel. Now Caliban suggests (a notion prefigured in Prospero's opening monologue) that in honest struggle and the recognition of limitations, the truth might perhaps be glimpsed, though it can never be approached by those who think to grasp it confidently by their own power. "Beating about for some large loose image to define" the experience, recorded in *The Tempest*, of the disillusion of magic and the acceptance of bounds, Caliban finally settles on this: "the greatest grandest opera rendered by a very provincial touring company indeed" (443). Paradoxically, it is the very poverty and ineptitude of the production that makes it valuable to its actors, for even though "there was not a single aspect of our whole performance, not even the huge stuffed bird of happiness, for which a kind word could, however patronisingly, be said," nevertheless it is "at this very moment [that] we do at last see ourselves as we are." And, more important, "for the first time in our lives we hear . . . the real Word which is our only *raison d'etre*"(443–44). At the moment when all pretense to aesthetic achievement helplessly falls away, and the actors are confronted with the authentic selves which they had used their performances to escape, they come to see God precisely in their distance from Him:

> we are blessed with that Wholly Other Life from which we are sepa-
> rated by an essential emphatic gulf of which our contrived fissures of
> mirror and proscenium arch—we understand them at last—are feebly
> figurative signs . . . it is just here, among the ruins and the bones, that
> we may rejoice in the perfected Work which is not ours.   (444)

It is just when the would-be proximity of mimetic art to truth fails that the distance of analogy, with its "feebly figurative signs," manages somehow to succeed. M. H. Abrams (following Yeats) presents us with the choice between mirror and lamp: Auden chooses the mirror, but is not content until he can make it clear that the mirror is a poor one indeed. "For now we see through a glass darkly." The one great principle of Auden's aesthetic is *humility*.[12]

The necessity of this principle is guaranteed by a greater principle, that of God as the Wholly Other. The "essential emphatic gulf" between God and man is bridged by Christ, but can be bridged in no other way. As Paul Ricoeur would argue later, Auden insists (again in an essay) that "the imagination is to be regarded as a natural faculty the subject matter of which is the phenomenal world, not its creator. For a poet brought up in a Christian society, it is perfectly possible to write a poem on a Christian theme, but when he does so, he is concerned with it as an aspect of a religion, that is to say, a human cultural fact, like other facts, not as a matter of faith. The poet is not there to convert the world" (*Secondary Worlds* 120–21).[13] The Incarnation makes poetry as a vehicle of the sacred—which for Blake, Wordsworth, Shelley, Keats it most certainly is—not only unnecessary but blasphemous. Auden is not the only Christian poet to take this stance: J. Hillis Miller argues, compellingly, that it is in essence the position that Gerard Manley Hopkins eventually reaches. Late in his career, "the writing of poetry seems to Hopkins neither right nor wrong; it is insignificant, like a talent for billiards or cricket" (*Disappearance* 334). Or, if you prefer, "Poetry makes nothing happen."

But is there any reason to write a poetry which can make nothing happen? In Auden's case, this question is particularly challenging, for his Christian belief that all gifts are to be placed in the service of God is accompanied by a profound conviction (which, incidentally, he shares with Samuel Johnson) that poetry of direct religious experience is inappropriate and, in the strict sense, impossible.[14] What Auden seems to be left with then, is a forcefully articulated refutation of Romanticism but no clear alternative to it, no way to relate his poetic vocation to his Christian faith. This is a particularly ironic situation, for it suggests that Romanticism, having (as Abrams has shown in *Natural Supernaturalism*) co-opted and transformed the language and the categories of Christianity, leaves the genuine Christian poet who rejects the Romantic movement speechless.

How Auden came to resolve this dilemma has, in its outlines, been clearly established: he would go on to develop (in Nathan Scott's words) a "poetry of civic virtue" and a poetics to complement it. Edward Mendelson describes this move as the replacement of the Romantic conception of "vatic poetry" with an older conception of "civic poetry," that is, a notion of art that emphasizes the artist's responsibilities as a citizen. Thus, in the conclusion of his only direct study of Romanticism, *The Enchafèd Flood*, Auden argues that we live in a new age for which "the heroic image is not the nomad wanderer through the desert or over the ocean [a reference to book 5 of Wordsworth's *Prelude*], but the less exciting figure of the builder, who renews the ruined walls of the city" (154).[15]

The poet is not a legislator, but rather a servant of the City—a word which means many things to Auden (as it did to Charles Williams, from whom he got it in that portentously capitalized form), but especially connotes at one and the same time the human community in general and the community of faith that God is building on earth through each person. "A community is comprised of n members united, to use a definition of Saint Augustine's, by a common love of something other than themselves," he writes (DH 64). And often—notably as the epigraph to "Memorial for the City"—he quotes a line from Dame Julian of Norwich that he discovered in Williams's *The Descent of the Dove*: "In the self-same point that our soul is made sensual, in the self-same point is the City of God ordained to him from without beginning" (see Charles Williams 224).

As I said, the thematic consequences for Auden's poetry of this turn toward civic poetry have been noted; but there are also certain practical, technical consequences that involve the generic means by which this poetry of citizenship can be brought to the contemporary audience. A key element of Auden's strategy for establishing his role as a servant of the City is his turn to occasional poetry. For the Romantic poet or the aesthete, to write poetry dictated by an occasion is to prostitute the imagination; for Auden, to refuse such a task is to succumb to arrogance. Thus he writes epithalamia and poems in memoriam (the latter genre he had embarked upon for the first time in 1939, just before his conversion, with poems on Yeats, Ernst Tollner, and Freud); he seems to relish the opportunity to provide poems for public occasions, like "Under Which Lyre," the 1946 Phi Beta Kappa poem at Harvard, or "Music is International," for the same organization at Columbia in 1947. Furthermore, most of his significant poems are now written for or presented to his friends: for example, each of the seven "Bucolics," and each of the twelve poems in "Thanksgiving for a Habitat," bears a dedication. In his inaugural lecture as Oxford's Professor of Poetry in 1956, he raises this issue lightly and wittily, wishing that "the duties of the Professor of Poetry were to produce, as occasion should demand, an epithalamium for the nuptials of a Reader in Romance languages, an elegy on a deceased Canon of Christ Church, a May-day masque for Somerville or an election ballad for his successor" (DH 31–32). It would be a mistake to think that he was merely joking: Auden was writing just such poems (see, for example, "Eleven Occasional Poems," [CP 751ff.]).

These paeans to the city, these eager embraces of poetic tasks set by others or set by the poet on behalf of others, clearly strive for a vital alternative to vatic poetry and aestheticism. But there is something sadly belated about Auden's effort, for not only have his fellow artists accepted the premises of vatic poetry, so has society as a whole. In some measure this may be attributed to the rhetorical force of the Romantic aesthetic, but more important are the drastic changes in Western society since the eighteenth century: there are practical and material reasons why poets have no alternative to social autonomy. No kings or aristocratic patrons support poets and give them tasks; there is no practical use for poetry in the modern world. Auden understood this perfectly well and wrote about it eloquently: the arts are now utterly gratuitous, and all modern attempts to "combine the gratuitous and the utile, to fabricate something which shall be both functional and beautiful," fail miserably (DH 74–75).

One interesting consequence for Auden of this lamentable state of affairs is that, in the latter part of his career, he finds himself tempted by one of the strands of Romanticism which in *The Sea and the Mirror* he had so violently rejected. There was never any danger, I think, of Auden coming to resemble Shelley.[16] But he did, in a curious way, come to resemble Wordsworth. Though Caliban heaps scorn on the Wordsworthian desire for an innocent past, Auden nevertheless returns again and again to his own version of same mythology. In poems and essays written throughout the fifties, Auden consistently presents himself as (in his terms) an Arcadian among Utopians, a dreamer of Eden in a world dominated by those who would build the New Jerusalem in our green and pleasant land.

Sometimes—as in "Dingley Dell and the Fleet," an essay in *The Dyer's Hand*—he describes the two tendencies evenhandedly: "Eden is a place where its inhabitants may do whatever they like to do; the motto over its gate is, 'Do what thou wilt is here the Law.' New Jerusalem is a place where its inhabitants like to do whatever they ought to do, and its motto is, 'In His will is our peace'" (DH 409). The rhetorical balance of the passage allows for no taking of sides. But in "Vespers," the fifth of his "Horae Canonicae," he boldly announces his allegiance. At dusk in "our city," the poem's Arcadian speaker meets his Utopian "Anti-type"; however,

Neither speaks. What experience could we possibly share?

Glancing at a lampshade in a store window, I observe it is too hideous for anyone in their senses to buy: He observes it is too expensive for a peasant to buy.

Passing a slum child with rickets, I look the other way: He looks the other way if he passes a chubby one.   (CP 637)

The playful tone of the poem should not obscure the underlying seriousness of its theme: "You can see, then, why, between my Eden and his New Jerusalem, no treaty is negotiable" (638). In poetic terms, this is a confrontation between the humble civic poets that Auden would call, in a later poem, the Horatians, and the arrogant Shelleyan legislators; and all the available evidence suggests that the legislators are winning the day. Auden is by nature a Horatian, and only by circumstance an Arcadian: he looks toward the past, or an imaginative vision of the past (in this poem he arrives in Eden by closing his eyes) only because he cannot realize his vision of poetry in the waking world of the present. But circumstance is an irresistible force to those who must live in historical time: thus this Arcadianism could be escaped by nothing less than a metamorphosis of personality. As he writes in "Dingley Dell," which echoes "Vespers" in several ways, "I suspect that between the Arcadian whose favorite daydream is of Eden, and the Utopian whose favorite daydream is of New Jerusalem there is a characterological gulf as unbridgeable as that between Blake's Prolifics and Devourers" (DH 409).[17]

But this is not the poem's conclusion. While this irreconcilable clash of anti-types may be the fate of certain individuals in the city, it is not necessarily the fate of the city itself; and "Vespers" concludes by assuming the city's perspective. It may be, muses the speaker, that this twilit meeting, far from being an accident, is "a rendezvous between two accomplices," each of whom reminds the other "of that half of their secret which he would most like to forget." For "a fraction of a second" each remembers "our victim," a victim both human and innocent, whose blood enables the "secular wall" of the city "safely [to] stand." This victim—Auden says "call him Abel, Remus, whom you will, it is one Sin Offering" (CP 639), but these are clearly shadowy types of Christ—in his innocence recalls the unspoiled perfection of Eden, the restoration of which is now the city's hope and goal; but this restoration is only made possible by the shedding of that very innocent's blood, for as the author of the Epistle to the Hebrews says, "without the shedding of blood there is no remission of sin" (9:22). Thus the Cross of Christ marks for Auden the focus of history, looking before and after to the perfection at either end of time, and in the process giving today's human striving context and meaning.

"Vespers" is a central poem in the Auden canon because in it he confronts and acknowledges his Arcadian and Wordsworthian tendencies while at the same time recognizing their limitations and hence their flaws. He can accept both truths in the faith that, while the community must strive for and in the end exemplify the wholeness incarnated in the God-man Christ, its individual members can never do so. Thus he manages to overcome the Prosperian temptation, which is, not to be partial, but to believe—in Prospero's case until it is *almost* too late—that such partiality can be made whole.[18]

In essence, Auden understands that he is obliged to resist his aesthetic sensibilities, no matter how powerfully they draw him, when they are in conflict with his ethical and religious convictions. In his "commonplace book," *A Certain World*, he recalls a decision he made as a child: in building an imaginary mine, he had to choose between two types of buddle (a device for washing ore), one of which was more beautiful, the other more efficient. "At this point I realized that it was my moral duty to sacrifice my aesthetic preference to reality or truth" (425).[19] Such resistance is a matter of continual and conscious will, for as Auden's spiritual master Kierkegaard says, purity of heart is to will one thing. But such acts of will force us to consider one final irony: do not the career and the writings of Kierkegaard show, does not his philosophy of existential choice demonstrate, that Romantic individualism, as a logical extension of the Protestant epistemology, is the only form of believing available to the modern mind? Is not Auden's rejection of his Romantic forebears a very Romantic thing to do?

It is often suggested that Romanticism, like the "inward turn" of Protestantism which spawned it, is ultimately irreversible. Even those who would reject it must do so on its terms, not on their own. This is the argument first articulated, I believe, by Robert Langbaum in *The Poetry of Experience* nearly forty years ago: "For it is not this or that political, philosophical, religious or even aesthetic commitment that marks the romanticist. It is the subjective ground of his commitment, the fact that he never forgets his commitment has been chosen" (21). And can this subjectivity be escaped? "Are not, after all, even our new classicisms and new Christian dogmatisms really romanticisms in an age which simply cannot supply the world-views such doctrines depend on, so that they become, for all their claims to objectivity, merely another opinion, the objectification of someone's personal view?" (28)

With this Auden would not agree. It may be that he never forgets that his commitment to civic poetry, and to Christianity, is chosen; but "private judgment is a meaningless term," he writes in his introduction to the anthology *The Protestant Mystics*, "for no one is omniscient and omnipotent and every man derives most of his thoughts, opinions and principles from others. Obedience to some authority is inescapable; if we reject the authority of tradition, we must accept the authority of local fashion" (F&A 51). To think of Romanticism as "local fashion" is not to diminish its achievements: rather, it is to recognize that those achievements grow out of individual choices that were made precisely in order to escape the constrictions of tradition and indeed of any kind of authority external to the choosing mind. For Auden, Romanticism may produce impressive edifices, but their foundations are of sand. In thinking of himself as a contemplative ruminating on the fate of the City, he sought to reach back beyond Romanticism to a long and deeply rooted tradition of poetics and moral inquiry. Only this tradition, in Auden's view, could make poetry fully modern because only this tradition could make poetry responsible to the world in which its practitioners must live and for which they should be thankful. As he writes in "The Horatians,"

"We can only
do what it seems to us we were made for, look at
    this world with a happy eye
    but from a sober perspective." (CP 773)

Seamus Heaney, speaking on this matter for the Larkin-Jarrell school of Auden studies, feels that Auden's later poetry wants to "comfort like a thread of wool rather than shock like a bare wire" (124). Certainly there is little attempt to shock in the poetry I have described, but neither is there much in it that is comforting or easy to swallow. In fact, in seeking to reclaim and revivify the tradition of civic poetry, Auden was making as difficult a choice as a modern poet could make. As Alasdair MacIntyre has written, "the project of founding a form of social order in which individuals could emancipate themselves from the contingency and particularity of tradition" has itself become a tradition, virtually a cult of what Auden calls "private judgment"; and it is not just *a* tradition, but "*the* project of modern liberal, individualist society" (*Whose* 335; italics mine). "To be educated into the culture of a liberal social order," says MacIntyre, is "characteristically to become the kind of person to whom it appears normal that a variety of goods should be pursued, each appropriate to its own sphere, with no overall good supplying any overall unity to life" (337). It is just this partiality of vision which Auden, in his reflections upon the City and in his resistance to his own Prosperian tendencies, seeks to overcome. If Auden's distaste for Romanticism is a feature of his career from the beginning, it was only in the war years that he achieved a sufficiently complex and sophisticated understanding of the inevitable failures of both major strands of Romanticism; and this understanding, in turn, prompted him to recover ancient and neglected ways of thinking about poetry and the polis. Auden would come to think that there is one poetic tradition for which communitarian reflection is not only possible, but essential.

CHAPTER 3

The Horatians

No civil style survived
That pandaemonium
But the wry, the sotto-voce,
Ironic and monochrome:
And where should we find shelter
For joy or mere content
When little was left standing
But the suburb of dissent.
                    —"WE TOO HAD KNOWN GOLDEN HOURS"

Near the end of the previous chapter I began to explore an old poetic tradition, the one identified with Horace, that Auden sought to reclaim as the most potent alternative to Romanticism. That reclamation project now must be explored in more detail, and the best way to conduct such an exploration is to run backwards through literary history because Auden took many years to recognize Horace as his proper model and only reached that understanding by thinking his way through the limitations of his modernist predecessors, evaluating his response to the nineteenth-century poets he admired, and then working further back through poetry's evolution. Auden's recognition of the poetic tradition to which he properly belonged grew and became more specific as he reflected upon first Byron, then Pope, and, much later, Horace himself. The emergence of that recognition needs to be traced.

Auden was never a social outsider in the sense that, say, Pope (in various ways) was. But he certainly felt himself, like Pope, to be in a kind of rebellion against his cultural and intellectual environment. In this of course he was no different from his fellow poets and intellectuals, for whom an adversarial stance was *de rigeur*. But Auden seems to have been more aware than his fellow poets of the need to rebel, if in a relatively mild way, against his High Modernist predecessors' too-narrow conception of poetic tradition. Auden may have been, in Paul Fussell's terms, a Modern rather than a Modernist poet, working "without any irritable need to quarrel with the past" (212)—but only if we think of the distant or long-term past. Fussell says of Modern poets—in which category he includes, along with Auden, such figures as Robert Frost, Edwin Muir, and Elizabeth Bishop—that "Disdain for their literary forebears is not their stock in trade, and they can produce their art without strenuous adversary gestures toward either the past or a present which differs from them in some of its critical opinions." On the whole I think this is a right and valuable point, but Harold Bloom is also right when he claims that the truly major poet must clear some imaginative space for himself or herself and that an essential element in this clearing out is the identification of the limitations and errors of the poet's great predecessors. Though never openly and perhaps not consciously, Auden firmly sets himself apart from Yeats and Eliot. This can well be seen in Auden's claim that the "three greatest influences" on his work were Dante, Langland, and Pope ("Criticism" 132) and in his recurrent praise of Thomas Hardy as his "first Master," that is, the first poet upon whose work he patterned his own (DH 38).

Auden was, of course, profoundly influenced by Yeats—though his response to Yeats was always ambivalent.[1] But Yeats has nothing to say about any of the figures Auden claimed as his masters, Dante alone excepted; and Yeats seems interested in Dante chiefly in order to compare him unfavorably to Blake.[2] In openly claiming such figures as his chief influences, Auden clearly sought to distance himself from Yeats, or at least from the poetic tradition in which Yeats works.

Eliot is if anything a more important figure for Auden. The focus of Eliot's attention, of course, rested on the seventeenth century, first emphasizing Donne; later Lancelot Andrewes and the Elizabethan dramatists; later still Dryden, for whom he had cultivated an early distaste that he later repudiated vigorously (for a description of this change, see Bush 114–15). But Pope, about whom he had next to nothing to say in his long career as a critic, was clearly beyond the pale. (It is interesting to note than, among Eliot's voluminous collected critical writings, there is only one essay on a poet who lived between Dryden and Blake, and that one is on Dr. Johnson.) Moreover, even though Eliot and Auden share a love of Dante, one does not have to look into their respective work very deeply to see that their Dantes are very different indeed. About Hardy, who was after all a Victorian, Eliot needed to say nothing.

So Auden in identifying his poetic tradition(s) was quite clearly setting himself at odds with his immediate predecessors in order to revise their understanding of literary history. The whole revision is significant, of course, but some of it constitutes a bit of a smoke screen. The influence of Hardy upon Auden's early work is clearly potent, especially in the younger poet's general tone of world-weariness and his imitation of Hardy's exceptional metrical and formal variety. (One can see this influence in the recently published *Juvenilia*, along with much Eliotic verse as well.) But pity the critic who would try to establish a meaningful connection between Auden's work and *Piers Plowman*.[3] And Dante seems to have influenced him chiefly by encouraging his tendency to imagine infernal scenes—as, for example, in "Caliban to the Audience." There is in Auden's verse, as far as I know, no stylistic imitation of Dante such as we see in the famous second section of "Little Gidding."

The Pope question deserves more attention. But that connection is not so obvious either, or not as obvious as one might at first think. Auden is clearly moving in what one might call a Popean direction as early as 1936, when he writes his "Letter to Lord Byron," since Byron is the one major Romantic poet dedicated to sustaining the eighteenth-century traditions of satirical narrative verse, and almost equally dedicated to ignoring the developments made by his contemporaries. It is not surprising, then, to find Auden, four years after his missive to Byron, writing a "New Year Letter" which appears to be directly modeled on Pope's epistles, not only in its evident genre but even in some of its typographical conventions (for example, the printing of proper names in an alternative typeface, in this case small capitals: "And SCHUBERT sang and MOZART played," etc.). But on closer inspection some interesting deviations from the model appear —indeed, some such deviations require very little inspection: it is immediately evident that Auden has, for no reason stated or obvious, abandoned the one poetic trait most characteristic of Pope, his use of iambic pentameter. The "New Year Letter" is indeed in couplets, like almost all of Pope's verse, but its meter is tetrameter.

What makes this deviation more interesting is that Auden had already swerved similarly once before, in his poem to Byron, which early on provides an apology to its addressee:

Ottava Rima would, I know, be proper,
    The proper instrument on which to pay
My compliments, but I should come a cropper;
    Rhyme-royal's difficult enough to play.   (CP 85)

It is hard to know how seriously to take this demurral. It is true that Auden had never yet embarked on a project of this kind, one that required him to write at considerable length—over a thousand lines— in a single meter. (He had previously written great amounts of verse for his plays, but they could be in all kinds of forms and meters, and no section had to be very long.) Moreover, this "Letter" began as something of a lark, intended to occupy some of the down time during his visit to Iceland (*Letters* 139–40). Yet Auden had already demonstrated such an astonishing facility in verse-crafting that it is difficult to credit his claim that he was not up to the demands even of Byron's challenging ottava rima. It may be that what we are witnessing here, and in the "New Year Letter", is Auden's persistent tendency— there are few more persistent in the course of his life—to establish a distance between himself and those he admired.

Auden was always quick to praise, but rarely did his praise lack qualification. His passion for Tolkien's *Lord of the Rings* was great, but he once paused to note that certain elements of the book's implicit theology are heretical. Though he admired the poetry of Charles Williams to a degree hard for most of us to understand, he was perfectly aware of Williams's rather severe limitations. Greatly though he loved Hardy, he knew that Hardy was not in the first rank of poets. Even Kierkegaard, whose reputation in England and America he did so much to boost, could occasionally receive his chastisement.[4]

This mixture of praise and censure may also be found in Auden's comments on Pope. "He was a snob and a social climber," Auden wrote in 1937,

> who lied about his ancestry and cooked his correspondence; he was fretful and demanded constant attention, he was sly, he was mean, he was greedy, he was vain, touchy, and worldly while posing as being indifferent to the world and to criticism; he was not even a good conversationalist.
>
> As a poet, he was limited to a single verse-form, the end-stopped couplet; his rare attempts at other forms were failures. To limitation of form was added limitation of interest. He had no interest in nature as we understand the term, no interest in love, no interest in abstract ideas, and none in Tom, Dick, and Harry. Yet his recognition was immediate, and his reputation never wavered during his lifetime. ("Pope" 90)

Auden goes on not only to explain the high valuation of Pope's poetry he refers to in that last sentence, but also to express his concurrence with it: "There are places in Pope, as in all poets, where his imagination is forced, where one feels a division between the object and the word, but at his best there are few poets who can rival his fusion of vision and language" (105). Further, Auden finds the celebrated translation of Homer no more than "a set task, honourably executed"; Pope "is at his best only when he is writing directly out of his own experience. . . . [S]how him the drawing-rooms where he longed to be received as a real gentleman, let him hear a disparaging remark about himself, and his poetry is beyond praise" (107).

Beyond praise. Auden maintained this high opinion of Pope throughout his life; if anything it intensified as the years went by. In 1969, reviewing Peter Quennell's account of Pope's early career, he concludes with these words: "As I get older and the times get gloomier and more difficult, it is to poets like Horace and Pope that I find myself more and more turning for the kind of refreshment I require" (F&A 124). (As though he had not turned to Pope with any frequency before.) Yet even a careful and historically literate reader of Auden's poetry would not be likely, minus the information just accumulated, to identify Pope as a shaping force for Auden. Pope's lack of interest in "abstract ideas" certainly is not characteristic of Auden, in whose poetry ideas are constantly engaged by him and engaging one another. Pope's adherence to a single verse form could not be further from the practice of Auden, who claimed, wrongly, to have written a poem in every known meter (see, e.g., Orlan Fox in Spender, *Tribute* 175) and whose formal variety can scarcely be matched in English poetry. Moreover, while Auden is certainly one of the funniest of modern poets, and often engages in satire, he is utterly without Pope's determination to respond, often with redoubled fierceness, to any and every personal attack. Auden seems never to have responded to attacks on his poetry or character, even though at points in his career, especially in the war years, such attacks could be quite common.[5] And even Auden's satire is far more gentle and self-deprecatory than Pope ever sought to be—for instance, in "Under Which Lyre," where his disapproval of certain scientistic and managerial trends in American culture takes the form of a sly "Hermetic decalogue," whose commands— including "Thou shalt not write thy doctor's thesis / On education," "Thou shalt not sit / With statisticians nor commit / A social science," and "Thou shalt not be on friendly terms / With guys in advertising firms" (CP 339)—seem too gentle to be Popean; the author of *The Dunciad* would scarcely have been so reluctant to name his enemies or to enumerate their personal eccentricities and vices. Nor can one imagine Pope doing what Auden does in the "Vespers" section of the "Horae Canonicae", which is, as we saw in chapter 2, to divide the satire equally between the poet and his temperamental opposite (his "Anti-type") and to assert both as valuable citizens of the *polis*.

If there is something elusive and ambiguous about Auden's relationship to Pope, might it be relevant that there is something equally elusive and ambiguous about Pope's relationship to the poetic predecessor with whom he claimed affiliation, Horace? It is well known that some of Pope's most accomplished poems are his "Imitations of Horace"; it is almost equally well known that these "imitations" draw extraordinarily little on their purported model. Moreover, in the epilogue to his *Satires* Pope implicitly condemns Horace for his over-politeness, his pusillanimity, and his obsequiousness towards the Augustan regime—all by having a dim-witted interlocutor praise Horace for just these traits (Pope 688)—and places himself firmly in the more aggressive Juvenalian camp of satirists. It is easy to imagine Juvenal, impossible to imagine Horace, saying what Pope says near the end of his epilogue: "I must be proud to see / Men not afraid of God, afraid of me" (701).

In making such comments Pope was merely inheriting Dryden's verdict on Horace ("a Temporizing Poet, a well Manner'd Court Slave . . . Who is ever decent, because he is naturally servile") and corresponding preference for Juvenal ("His thoughts are sharper, his Indignation against Vice is more vehement");[6] but why, then, did Pope claim to be imitating Horace instead? Maynard Mack has plausibly suggested that Pope, as a Catholic in a period of intermittently severe anti-Catholic prejudice, did not wish to associate himself with a seditious poet (563). (Fourth-century biographies of Juvenal, none of which have any discernible authority but all of which were accepted as generally true in Pope's time, claimed that Juvenal had been exiled by Hadrian or Domitian as punishment for some scurrility about an imperial favorite [Rudd x–xi].)

How much Auden knew of this curious episode in the history of poetic influence cannot be ascertained. It may be no more than coincidence that his own links with Pope reveal a similar swerve, but it is indeed the case that, just as Pope claimed adherence to the Horatian tradition when his real allegiances lay with Juvenal, so Auden claimed to be a follower of Pope when in fact his poetry much more closely resembles that of Horace. His kinship with Horace may be something of which Auden only gradually became aware, for what we see in his work (as I suggested at the beginning of this chapter) is a kind of working back along the lines of the Horatian tradition, from Byron back through Pope and eventually to Horace himself. It was only late in Auden's career that he made explicit his homage to Horace and the tradition that Horace begot.

First Horace himself, and then that tradition. The personal similarities between Horace and Auden are striking to say the least. Horace is bisexual, Auden homosexual. Each evidences a liking, especially in youth, for obscenity. In one of his early satires (1:4) Horace wonders whether his poetry is *sermoni propriora*, too prosy, too much like talk; Auden once told his friend Elizabeth Mayer, speaking of his later and consciously Horatian poetry, that he was trying "to keep the diction and prosody within a hairsbreadth of being prose without becoming it" (Carpenter 419). Each poet tends pronouncedly towards satire in his early work but mellows later and produces as much self-criticism as criticism of others. Celebratory and grateful poems dominate the later work of each poet; the emphasis on gratitude can be seen particularly clearly in Horace's poetry about his Sabine farm and Auden's about his house in Kirchstetten. Both poets lived alternately in the country and the city, and articulated their concern for the future of the city from a distant and leisured perspective.[7]

Auden's later poetry is increasingly filled with echoes of Horace, and some of his poems seem directly derived from Horatian originals.[8] For instance, Auden's last major poetic sequence, "Thanksgiving for a Habitat" (most of which was written from 1962 to '64), owes a great deal to Horace's poems about his Sabine farm, especially the most famous of them, *"Hoc erat in votis"* (*Satires* 2:6). Horace's anticipation of a return to his farm, and the subsequent good meals and fine conversation with friends, find their response in the sections of "Thanksgiving" about friendship ("For Friends Only") and an evening meal in the dining room ("Tonight at Seven-Thirty"). Indeed, some passages in "Thanksgiving" come near to translation of Horace's poem. For instance, this is how Horace commences:

> This was what I had prayed for: a small piece of land
> With a garden, a fresh flowing spring of water at hand
> Near the house, and, above and behind, a small forest stand.
> But the gods have done much better for me, and more—
> It's perfect. I ask nothing else, except to implore,
> O Son of Maia, that you make these blessings my own
> For the rest of my life. (*Satires* 138)

And here are the corresponding passages from the second section of "Thanksgiving":

> I, a transplant
>
> from overseas, at last am dominant
>   over three acres and a blooming
> conurbation of country lives . . .
> . . . .
>   what I dared not hope or fight for
> is, in my fifties, mine, a toft-and-croft
>   where I needn't, ever, be at home *to*
>
> those I am not at home *with*, not a cradle,
>   a magic Eden without clocks,
> and not a windowless grave, but a place
>   I may go both in and out of. (CP 689–91)

Among Auden's many poems in the Horatian mode, one which echoes his Roman counterpart especially clearly is, as one might expect, "The Horatians," a poem which, among other things, makes for a fascinating case study in intertextuality. Into Horace's mouth, and the mouths of his "descendants," Auden places a comparison with one of the greatest of poets:

> "As makers go,
>   compared with Pindar or any
> of the great foudroyant masters who don't ever
> amend, we are, for all our polish, of little
>   stature. . . ." (773)

This disavowal of competition with Pindar is not merely Auden's imposition upon Horace, for in one of his Odes (*"Pindarum quisquis,"* IV:2) Horace does the same:

> Whoever attempts to emulate Pindar, Julus,
> depends from wings that are fastened with wax
> by Daedalian art and shall give his name
>   to some glassy sea. (*Complete* 179)

This is interesting in light of both Auden's repeated warnings against the hubris with which artists are afflicted and his well-known poem about Icarus, or rather Breughel's painting of Icarus ("Musée des Beaux Arts," CP 146). It is easy to see how for Auden Breughel's Icarus could become an emblem of artistic pride, not only because (like Lucifer) he falls, but because no one except God notices: Auden never tired of insisting that the social and political history of Europe would be exactly the same had its greatest artists never lived (see, e.g., EA 393). Horace and Auden alike wish to avoid that pride—though to be sure Horace had, or at least openly articulated, a greater faith in the lasting power of his poetry than Auden ever did. To belong to the Horatian tradition is to eschew the temptations and the dangers of Pindaric ambition.

Auden is clearly aware in "The Horatians" that the tradition he describes has few if any significant adherents among poets. Having been raised on the Romantic traditions described in the previous chapter, Auden's poetic contemporaries seem scarcely aware of the Horatian alternative, and therefore the Horatians of which Auden speaks are not necessarily poets or artists:

> Among those I really know, the
> British branch of the family, how many have
> found in the Anglican church
> your Maecenas who enabled
>
> a life without cumber, as pastors adjective
> to rustic flocks, as organists in trollopish
> cathedral towns. (CP 772)

If Auden has anyone specifically in mind here, it is certainly Sydney Smith, the nineteenth-century writer, priest, and wit who was one of his heroes and who provided for him a motto which he repeatedly used, most notably at the end of "Under Which Lyre": "take short views" (CP 339). (In a letter to a friend suffering from depression, Smith gave a series of recommendations which included "2. Short views of human life—not further than dinner or tea" [F&A 153]). Smith was a lover of city life who, as a result of the Clergy Residence Bill of 1808, was forced to become a real, not just a nominal, country parson. To his surprise, he eventually came to find his life agreeable, especially after he was named Canon of St. Paul's Cathedral, and was able late in life to write these unmistakably Horatian words:

> Being Canon of St. Paul's in London, and a rector of a parish in the country, my time is divided equally between town and country. . . . I dine with the rich in London, and physic the poor in the country; passing from the sauces of Dives to the sores of Lazarus. I am, upon the whole, a happy man, have found the world an entertaining place, and am thankful to Providence for the part allotted to me in it. (quoted in F&A 157)

But Smith was also an able controversialist and was constantly involved in one polemic or another; and therefore the words which close Auden's "The Horatians" apply to him as well as to Horace and to Auden himself:

> "We can only
> do what it seems to us we were made for, look at
> this world with a happy eye
> but from a sober perspective." (CP 773)

But this vision of poetic purpose can only seem, to the Romantic and the Modernist poet alike—and, perhaps equally important, to the readers of poetry who have absorbed their self-valuation—unacceptably constricting and limiting.[9] Thus Auden finds himself in a difficult position: committed to the vocation of poet, yet convinced that the conditions under which one may write poetry in our society are ethically and politically dubious at best. Worse still, Auden's understanding of what it means to be a Christian poet—that is, a Christian whose profession is poetry—was dominated by an immense skepticism about the ability of language to designate and describe spiritual experience in a manner worthy of its subject:

> Poems, like many of Donne's and Hopkins's, which express a poet's personal feelings of religious devotion or penitence, make me uneasy. It is quite in order that a poet should write a sonnet expressing his devotion to Miss Smith because the poet, Miss Smith, and all his readers know perfectly well that, had he chanced to fall in love with Miss Jones instead, his feelings would be exactly the same. But if he writes a sonnet expressing his devotion to Christ, the important point, surely, is that his devotion is felt for Christ and not for, say, Buddha or Mahomet, and this point cannot be made in poetry; the Proper Name proves nothing. (DH 458)[10]

Elsewhere he argues, as one might expect from "Caliban to the Audience," that one may write about religious experience only as a cultural fact among other cultural facts, which is only part of what such experience is. Therefore such treatment is necessarily inaccurate and misleading (*Secondary Worlds* 120–21). And in his "Dichtung und Wahrheit (An Unwritten Poem)" (CP 647), Auden would retract his provisional acceptance of love poetry: he could not write a poem to his lover which would indicate without possibility of confusion that his love was for this particular individual and not for anyone else.

Given these arguments, it is rather surprising that Auden continued to write poetry at all. Nevertheless he did, but, as Lucy McDiarmid contends in her stimulating book *Auden's Apologies for Poetry*, under what one is tempted to call the sign of erasure. After his return to Christianity in 1940, writes McDiarmid, "Every major poem and

THE HORATIANS

every major essay became a *retractio*, a statement of art's frivolity, vanity and guilt" (x). "Deference, apology, self-deprecation—these become ritual gestures in Auden's later poetry. The lyrics written after 1948 [assume] that all poems . . . are silly and trivial. . . . The sounded note is one of perpetual apology" (120). Ultimately, McDiarmid argues, poetry for Auden becomes the realm of *play*, that logically indefensible but necessary and distinctive element of human culture. And indeed, "The Poet and the City" concludes by arguing that "among the half dozen or so things for which a man of honor should be prepared, if necessary, to die for, the right to play, the right to frivolity, is not the least" (DH 89).

Note, however, that this confession is not quite so abject as McDiarmid's argument would lead us to believe. If the right to play is something worth dying to preserve, then one need not be ashamed of admitting one's frivolity. McDiarmid acknowledges that in such statements Auden gives art a relatively high place in the hierarchy of values; but she goes on to insist that Auden can only justify such frivolity if it "invokes less frivolous realms" (xii)—which may well be Caliban's argument at the end of his monologue in *The Sea and the Mirror* (CP 444), but one which Auden notably does *not* make in "The Poet and the City." Elsewhere Auden seems to make it clear that the frivolous need not invoke anything else in order to justify its existence, but only must avoid arrogance: "Christianity draws a distinction between what is frivolous and what is serious, but allows the former its place. What it condemns is not frivolity but idolatry, that is to say, taking the frivolous seriously" (DH 430).

Ultimately McDiarmid may be attempting to force a false consistency on Auden. By that I do not mean that Auden's thought is inconsistent —in fact, after about 1945 it is so consistent as to be repetitious—but rather that it is not consistent in the way that McDiarmid thinks it is. Auden did not always demean poetry; he was capable of making some rather substantial claims for it but was exceptionally careful to adjust his claims and retractions to the context at hand.

McDiarmid explains one such context very well: Auden always made a point (as we have seen) of confessing poetry's inability to communicate absolute value; his frequent theme, in McDiarmid's words, is "the poet's incapacity to say anything worthy of the spiritual absolutes he can only name" (*Auden's Apologies* 126).[11] But McDiarmid does not consider sufficiently well another context for Auden's statements about poetry, the Romantic and modern claims for poetic autonomy or revolutionary power against which (as we have also seen) he reacted with special vehemence. Neglect of this point, and of the Horatian alternative Auden embraced, inclines McDiarmid to treat apologies and retractions conceived as correctives to poetic hubris as, instead, statements of absolute validity about the nature of poetry. Several of the great poems from the 1950s could be used to illustrate this point, but that now-familiar "Vespers" section of the "Horae Canonicae" does as well as any. McDiarmid argues that this poem, "more forcefully" than others in the sequence, "condemns all art as complicit in society's guilt," pointing to the speaker's confession that he looks the other way when "passing a slum child with rickets." She further argues that "by seeing his earnest radical counterpart, the Utopian, he is forced, he says, 'to remember our victim,' to have something spiritually significant brought home to him" (151). But this interpretation of the poem is based on the unwarranted assumption that one may equate the artist with Arcadianism. Auden in "Vespers" is writing about a temperamental division that may be seen anywhere, among any group of people; art has not taken up a single side in this perpetual conflict. If Auden condemns himself in "Vespers," as I believe he does, he condemns himself as an ordinary sinner and not as an artist per se.

But—to reverse the emphasis of my second chapter—he also condemns his Utopian "Anti-type," whose sins and errors mirror those of the poem's Arcadian speaker. McDiarmid's assertion that the radical Utopian functions to remind the Arcadian of the "spiritually significant" fails to attend to this crucial point: the twilit rendezvous is "forcing us *both*, for a fraction of a second, to remember our victim (but for him I could forget the blood, but for me he could forget the innocence)" (484; italics mine). *Both* positions, the Arcadian and the Utopian, deserve condemnation for their partiality of vision, their failure to recognize the whole truth. This apparently "fortuitous intersection of life-paths" is in truth a "rendezvous between two accomplices who, in spite of themselves, cannot resist meeting"; each seeks "to remind the other . . . of that half of their secret which he would most like to forget" (639). Let us not forget that the Utopian vision presented in this poem echoes the language of Stalin's Marxism and Hitler's National Socialism and that McDiarmid's "earnest radical" dreams, as Auden reminds us, of a time when "those he hates shall hate themselves instead." Auden is scarcely giving over the realm of spiritual significance to Utopian political visionaries.[12]

Again, both possess some part of the truth, and in their rendezvous the whole truth is made manifest—the whole truth, that is, about their victim ("call him Abel, Remus, whom you will, it is one Sin Offering") and the nature of his redemptive suffering: "For without a cement of blood (it must be human, it must be innocent) no secular wall will safely stand" (639). But where and how does this vital rendezvous, this meshing of half-truths, occur? In the poem, by courtesy of the poet. Auden the poet provides the necessary context for Auden the temperamentally Arcadian man; and that context is the City—or at least (see the quotation that prefaces this chapter) the "suburb of dissent."

The whole purpose of Auden's retractions and apologies is to demolish, ruthlessly if necessary, poetic pretensions. The poet as poet is neither a revolutionary nor a hero nor an autonomous artificer; but the poet may nevertheless serve the City as a *citizen*. McDiarmid says that Auden's later poetry undermines "any elevated notion of the poet's function in society" (*Auden's Apologies* 150) and that is clearly true. She lists among such "elevated" functions that notion that the poet "reminds the society of the values it might otherwise forget"; but that doesn't seem particularly elevated to me. Nor does it seem so to Auden, who devotes much of the last twenty years of his poetic life to just such reminding, to a gentle prodding of our consciences, to the subtlest of hints that all of us, poets and readers and everyone else, indeed belong to, and are responsible for, what the Franco-Polish poet Oscar Milosz called "the great human family."[13] This is the chief burden of Auden's Horatianism; that tradition does not disparage poetry, but rather situates it within a context of social responsibility.

CHAPTER 4

Local Culture

Whoever rules, our duty to the City
is loyal opposition, never greening
for the big money, never neighing after
    a public image.

Let us leave rebellions to the choleric
who enjoy them: to serve as a paradigm
now of what a plausible Future might be
    is what we're here for.

—"THE GARRISON"

One of the more interesting developments in recent American political and social thought has been the emergence of communitarianism—in large part because, though no one knows exactly what communitarianism is, people do tend to think good thoughts about the notion of community. As Wendell Berry writes, "Community is a concept, like humanity or peace, that virtually no one has taken the trouble to quarrel with; even its worst enemies praise it" (179). Perhaps some communitarians have chosen not to define their aims and goals too specifically, because they know that the cold light of specificity tends to dispel the warm fuzzy aura that surrounds that word "community."

But definitions have been risked. According to Christopher Lasch, communitarianism "proposes a general strategy of devolution or decentralization, designed to end the dominance of large organizations [this means multinational corporations as well as the U.S. government] and to remodel our institutions on a human scale" (62). Communitarians, then, inveigh against the old habit of thinking of the polity largely in national terms and advocate its replacement by more localized forms of attention.

A curious trait of communitarians is that few of them seem to have arrived at their position willingly. Rather, they have become communitarians only because more grandiose and universal systems (whether Marxism, old-fashioned liberalism, or state capitalism) have, in their view, failed us all. In this regard the paradigmatic communitarian is St. Francis of Assisi. After he discovered the Biblical principles on which he and his followers would base their brotherhood—by picking three verses at random from the Gospels—he sought again and again to bring his message to other parts of the known world. But each time he prepared to voyage forth to make his message universal, some barrier (whether a Pope's edict or the collapse of his health or God's unmediated will) would prevent him from leaving Italy; thus he was forced, until quite late in his career, to cultivate the Franciscan spirit of community only in his native Umbria. Like most communitarians, then, Francis became one by default. No one, it seems, wants *cultiver son jardin* as long as changing the world remains a viable option.

This is especially the case for intellectuals, because, as Karl Mannheim pointed out many years ago in his *Ideology and Utopia*, intellectuals in Western societies form a distinct social (if not a socio-economic) class "whose special task is to provide an interpretation of the world," to "play the part of watchmen in what otherwise would be a pitch-black night" (142, 143). An intellectual, then, by definition thinks globally rather than locally; so much so that to accept the validity of local concerns is to court excommunication from the church of the clerisy. This danger may best be seen, I think, in the example of Albert Camus. Think of some of his most controversial statements about the Algerian conflict in which his family was endangered: "I believe in justice, but I will defend my mother before justice" (quoted by Lottman 618). "If anyone . . . thinks heroically that one's brother must die rather than one's principles, I shall go no farther than to admire him from a distance. I am not of his stamp" (Camus 113). If the virulence with which such statements were repudiated by the French intelligentsia seems shocking today, that is only because in the intervening forty years we have lost confidence in the mental and moral detachment of the intellectual. Even if the detachment and objectivity of the intellectual is a fiction, it remains necessary to the very concepts of "intellectual" and "intelligentsia." To the adherents of that fiction, the celebration of local culture and local knowledge is anathema— though, it should be noted, Antonio Gramsci strove to envision a clan of "organic intellectuals" who would emerge from the people to become their champions on the field of mental strife (6). Such intellectuals would indeed arise from particular communities, but (given Gramsci's belief in the universal applicability of Marx's general analysis of the class struggle) they would all hold the same political convictions. Even the organic intellectual, then, is not local in an utterly particularistic sense.

These reflections apply quite directly to Auden. Though Auden settled on communitarian principles with great reluctance, after the defeat of his universalist hopes he articulated those principles with remarkable force and clarity. Moreover, he understood both the costs and benefits of choosing to cultivate local knowledge and local attachments better than almost any political thinker writing about such issues today. For that reason alone his work on this subject deserves our attention. But it also repays study because of certain conflicts into which Auden's particular brand of communitarianism drew him— conflicts that may have been inevitable.

What we need here is a vantage point from which to survey both the early and the later Auden, and that point is provided by "New Year Letter," the first long poem Auden wrote after he moved to America at the outset of the Second World War.[1] One of the most notable and surprising features of this poem is its celebration of local culture. Auden's conception of what local culture is and what it does develops throughout the "New Year Letter" but finds condensed expression near the beginning as Auden remembers a recent gathering of frie. at the home of Elizabeth Mayer (to whom this "letter" is written. After describing the various objects and actions which the sui observes with a "neutral eye" on earth, he writes that this same sun

Lit up America and on
A cottage in Long Island shone
Where BUXTEHUDE as we played
One of his *passacaglias* made
Our minds a *civitas* of sound
Where nothing but assent was found,
For art had set in order sense
And feeling and intelligence,
And from its ideal order grew
Our local understanding too.   (CP 200)

The phrase "ideal order" (though Auden does not acknowledge this in his notes to the poem) comes from T. S. Eliot's famous essay "Tradition and the Individual Talent": "The existing monuments [of European art] form an ideal order among themselves, which is modified by the introduction of the new (the really new) work of art among them" (*Selected* 5). But while Eliot's concerns are merely intertextual, content with describing how these "monuments" are organized and deployed in relation to one another, Auden's interests are markedly different: the question for him is, How does art help us (if indeed it does) to set our lives in order? For Eliot the ideal order is to be contemplated and celebrated; for Auden it is to be used. And it finds its use in the formation of "local understanding," of small groups of people united, if only temporarily, to become citizens of their own tiny republic.

Later in the poem, at the beginning of its third and last part, Auden returns to the same message:

And SCHUBERT sang and MOZART played
And GLUCK and food and friendship made
Our privileged community
That real republic which must be
The State all politicians claim,
Even the worst, to be their aim.   (CP 221)

I cite this passage too because otherwise it might not be clear how such an apparently high view of art's utility could be reconciled with that famous opinion Auden had pronounced for the first (but certainly not the last) time almost exactly a year before, in his famous elegy on Yeats: "poetry makes nothing happen" (CP 247). Does Auden now mean to say that if poetry can't make anything happen music can? There were certainly times in his later career when he came close to saying just that, but in the context of the "New Year Letter" the point is that art, while it cannot of its own power *enforce* any alteration of consciousness or morality, can *help* those who would be joined together to find their desired unity. Artists can never become the legislators of the world, acknowledged or unacknowledged, but they can become after a fashion public servants. Yet even this they can do successfully only if the public they serve is small enough for real commonality of purpose to be possible: art can promote "local understanding" in a miniature *civitas* but cannot change the world. And this is true not because art is weak, but because, in Auden's view in 1940, all dreams of universal or even national unity, dreams which he himself had tried for a decade to share in, are fundamentally absurd. Art serves local understanding only because it is the only kind of understanding available.

One of the more interesting points to be made about Auden's conclusion here is that he had been confronted with just such an example of perfect local understanding—an example even more perfect, and certainly far more dramatic, than he found in Elizabeth Mayer's Long Island home—less than seven years before, and had been unable to accept it. He did not provide a full account of the experience until 1964, thirty years after it had occurred, and even then he did not openly admit that the experience was his own. (It was part of his introduction to Anne Freemantle's anthology *The Protestant Mystics*.) The account needs to be quoted at some length:

> One fine summer night in June 1933 I was sitting on a lawn after dinner with three colleagues, two women and one man. . . . We were talking casually about everyday matters when, quite suddenly and unexpectedly, something happened. I felt myself invaded by a power which, though I consented to it, was irresistible and certainly not mine. For the first time in my life I knew exactly—because, thanks to the power, I was doing it—what it means to love one's neighbor as oneself. I was also certain, though the conversation continued to be perfectly ordinary, that my three colleagues were having the same experience. (In the case of one of them, I was later able to confirm this.) My personal feelings towards them were unchanged—they were still colleagues, not intimate friends—but I felt their existence as themselves to be of infinite value and rejoiced in it.
>
> I recalled with shame the many occasions on which I had been spiteful, snobbish, selfish, but the immediate joy was greater than the shame, for I knew that, so long as I was possessed by this spirit, it would be literally impossible for me deliberately to injure another human being. I also knew that the power would, of course, be withdrawn sooner or later and that, when it did, my greed and self-regard would return. The experience lasted at its full intensity for about two hours when we said good-night to each other and went to bed. When I awoke the next morning, it was still present, though weaker, and it did not vanish completely for two days or so. The memory of the experience has not prevented me from making use of others, grossly and often, but it has made it much more difficult for me to deceive myself about what I am up to when I do. And among the various factors which several years later brought me back to the Christian faith in which I had been brought up, the memory of this experience and asking myself what it could mean was one of the most crucial, though, at the time it occurred, I thought I had done with Christianity for good.   (F&A 69–70)

This story fits nicely with the celebration elaborated in "New Year Letter": here indeed is a tiny Athens, even a miniature New Jerusalem. But when Auden wrote a poem about the experience soon after it happened, his chief concern was to articulate his sense that the acceptance of such an excessively local culture was morally and politically indefensible.

The early stanzas of the poem, which Auden would eventually give the title "A Summer Night," show no sign of uneasiness:

> Equal with colleagues in a ring
> I sit on each calm evening
>   Enchanted as the flowers
> The opening light draws out of hiding
> From leaves with all its dove-like pleading,
>   Its logic and its powers.

> That later we, though parted then
> May still recall these evenings when
>   Fear gave his watch no look;
> The lion griefs loped from the shade
> And on our knees their muzzles laid,
>   And Death put down his book.   (FA 136–37)

But as the poem moves on its center of interest shifts: what about those who are not so fortunate as to be enclosed within such an Edenic "ring"? How does an acknowledgment of their existence affect the comfortable insiders? Or is life in such an enchanted circle dependent on a studied ignorance of those outside? Perhaps the insiders, "whom hunger cannot move,"

>   do not care to know,
> Where Poland draws her Eastern bow,
>   What violence is done;
> Nor ask what doubtful act allows
> Our freedom in this English house,
>   Our picnics in the sun.

The creepered wall stands up to hide
The gathering multitudes outside
   Whose glances hunger worsens;
Concealing from their wretchedness
Our metaphysical distress,
   Our kindness to ten persons.   (137)

This vision of love and community, then, may not be a free gift in which to rejoice, but a dangerous temptation to social quietism: it is at best a "doubtful act." What the Auden of 1964 celebrates as a blessed inability to harm others, the Auden of 1933 fears as an insidious tendency to be satisfied with one's "kindness to ten persons" while the "gathering multitudes" outside starve. The perfect local understanding which the Auden even of 1940 celebrates as an incalculable gift, the Auden of 1933 finds scandalous precisely because it is local and not universal.[2] It is only at the end of the poem, when "sounds of riveting" (138) betoken the rebuilding (presumably on more just and equitable foundations) of a ruined city, that the note of exaltation with which the poem began returns: exaltation becomes possible again only when the little collegial circle of friends becomes a new city. As Edward Mendelson writes in the richest and wisest reading of this great poem (I am giving his words a somewhat different emphasis than he does), "Personal love . . . will have power to calm nations and grant even the murderer forgiveness and peace" only when it is "transfigured into public concord" (*Early* 170).

How, then, did Auden get in less than seven years from the one position to the other? One might begin by describing his disillusionment with Marxism and his return to Christianity, a return which was not yet complete when "New Year Letter" was written but was nearly so. But we should be careful here. That Auden rejected Marxism and became a Christian is certainly true; but there is no necessary connection between Christianity and the embrace of local culture exemplified in "New Year Letter." In fact, it would be more accurate to say that Marxism and Christianity alike stand opposed to such localization of culture, which finds more sympathy in certain ancient Greek and Roman modes of cultural thought (Aristotle rather than Plato,

Horace rather than Virgil). The cultivation of "local understanding," as is manifest in the passages quoted from both "New Year Letter" and "A Summer Night," requires as an essential, perhaps *the* essential, component the cultivation of friendship—and friendship, while an Aristotelian virtue, tends to be suspect both to Marxism (which opposes to it the ideal of "comradeship") and to Christianity (which opposes to it the ideal of "brotherhood and sisterhood in Christ"). Jeremy Taylor, the seventeenth-century Anglican divine, wrote: "When friendships were the noblest things in the world, charity was little."[3] In other words, when the ancient Greeks and Romans emphasized the great virtue of friendship, they neglected to care for those who stood outside *philia*'s charmed circle, the "gathering multitudes" outside the "creepered wall." Likewise Samuel Johnson: "All friendship is prefer-ring the interest of a friend, to the neglect, or, perhaps, against the interest of others. . . . Now Christianity recommends universal benevo-lence, to consider all men as our brethren; which is contrary to the virtue of friendship, as described by the ancient philosophers" (Boswell 946). One might easily argue that Marxism inherits this Christian universalism, while proposing alternative explanations for its practical failure and alternative means for its eventual realization. Thus it is by no means obvious that Auden's embrace of Christianity would natu-rally lead to an embrace of local culture and local understanding.

In fact, it seems to me that Auden's return to Christianity and his celebration of local culture form two rather distinct movements in his intellectual life that meet at only one point, a point which we will soon identify. First, it is vital to note that at no point in Auden's intel-lectual development does he deny that human beings are capable of creating universal *evil*. For instance, from "New Year Letter":

> And more and more we are aware,
> However miserable may be
> Our parish of immediacy,
> How small it is, how, far beyond,
> Ubiquitous within the bond
> Of one impoverishing sky,
> Vast spiritual disorders lie.   (CP 205)

Then follows a catalogue of those "disorders," from China to Spain to Ethiopia to Poland. But a grave spiritual and moral danger, Auden argues, arises from the recognition of such universal evil. "Who," he asks,

> will not feel blind anger draw
> His thoughts toward the Minotaur,
> To take an early boat for Crete
> And rolling, silly, at its feet
> Add his small tidbit to the rest?
> It lures us all; even the best,
> *Les hommes de bonne volonté*, feel
> Their politics perhaps unreal
> And all they have believed untrue,
> Are tempted to surrender to
> The grand apocalyptic dream
> In which the persecutors scream
> As on the evil Aryan lives
> Descends the night of the long knives,
> The bleeding tyrant dragged through all
> The ashes of his capitol.   (206)

One might with cause assume that Auden here is arguing for pacifism, claiming that the attempt to defeat Hitler will reduce the Allies to Hitler's moral level. But Auden, though he felt the appeal of pacifism, never embraced it, and soon after writing "New Year Letter" explicitly rejected it.[4] Instead, Auden is warning the Allies that they are not immune to the forces that (as he wrote about Germany in "September 1, 1939") "have driven a culture mad" (SP 86); the great if not inevitable danger of fighting the Nazis is that one may become contaminated by the very disorder one sets out to cure. Thus the little parable that, in the notes which he originally appended to "New Year Letter," Auden attaches to the lines about throwing oneself at the feet of the Minotaur:

> During the last war Frau M was in Tübingen. Walking home one cloudy night, she met two professors from the university, carrying rifles.
>   "What's the matter?" she asked.

"There's an enemy aeroplane overhead. Can't you see its pilot-light?"
"But that's not an aeroplane. That's Jupiter." (*Double* 92)

Having thrown themselves at the feet of what Auden calls in *The Sea and the Mirror* "the Minotaur of Authority," (CP 438) these men have lost their ability to make elementary moral and even perceptual discriminations. And let us not fail to note that these are professors, a fact that indicates that Auden's warning is chiefly directed against the intellectuals, who are in the greatest danger of all because of their conviction that their detachment and objectivity place them beyond danger. This is a lesson, I believe, Auden learned in Spain, where he saw how the Republicans (surely *hommes de bonne volonté*), consumed with hatred for anything associated with the old regime, had closed and in many cases wrecked or burned the churches of Barcelona— and without eliciting recognition of their act, much less disapproval, from their supporters among the intelligentsia (*Modern* 41).

Perhaps Auden's insistence upon the nearly infinite human capacity for evil would not have been so objectionable to the intellectuals of his time were it not for his simultaneous insistence that humans lack an equal capacity for goodness. A consistent theme in Auden's work of this period is that we lack the power to *undo* the evil that we have the power to *do*. It is this belief that leads Auden to what would become one of the most persistent features of his poetry until his death: the praise of humility which was discussed in our second chapter's reflections on *The Sea and the Mirror*. This is the point at which his conversion to Christianity and his acceptance of the validity of local culture converge.

One of the first significant appearances of this leitmotif comes in Auden's great sonnet sequence of 1938, "In Time of War" (later revised and retitled "Sonnets from China"), which grew out of his and Christopher Isherwood's visit to China. In the last sonnet of the sequence, for instance, Auden describes the hopes for human perfection in a perfectly innocent past of what Eliot would call "unified sensibility" and in a perfectly ordered future—these being the dreams, as he would later write in "Vespers," of the Arcadian and the Utopian respectively. But here he calmly rejects both visions of perfection as being incompatible with the fundamental human condition:

> But we are articled to error; we
> Were never nude and calm like a great door,
>
> And never will be perfect like the fountains.... (EA 262)

A full understanding of this inevitable fallenness requires not only humility but a recognition of the historical value of humility: in the verse "Commentary" to the sequence Auden writes of the importance of giving "Our gratitude to the Invisible College of the Humble, / Who through the ages have accomplished everything essential" (268). Auden's conviction on this point finds its most perfect poetic expression about a year after the completion of "New Year Letter," in the penultimate (later, upon revision, to be the last) stanza of "At the Grave of Henry James":

> All will be judged. Master of nuance and scruple,
> Pray for me and for all writers, living or dead:
>   Because there are many whose works
> Are in better taste than their lives, because there is no end
> To the vanity of our calling, make intercession
>   For the treason of all clerks. (CP 312)

Julien Benda's famous indictment in *La Trahison des Clercs* (1927) is here transformed: "treason" becomes neither a crime to be expiated nor a sin to be overcome but rather the necessary condition of intellectual life.

Auden's humble recognition of the profundity of human evil-doing and the limited capacity for doing good has two major consequences for his thought: first, that the Christian belief in original sin and the concomitant need for divine salvation is, in all essentials, right; second, that one must do what one can, not what one wishes one could do, to make things better. In the famous phrase from "Tintern Abbey," Auden determines to cultivate and to praise "that best portion of a good man's life: / His little, nameless, unremembered acts / Of kindness and of love"; and from Sydney Smith he learns (as we have seen) to "take short views." This emphasis on limited aims, this desired reconciliation with inevitable incompetence, appears often in Auden's later poetry—to take but one example, in "Memorial for the City" (1949), in which a versified history of the failed Constantinian experiment of melding the City of Man with the City of God is followed by the voice of "our Weakness," a voice never acknowledged by the hubristic Constantinians whose best efforts culminated in the encompassing tyrannies of Hitler and Stalin (CP 591–96).

Auden's replacement for these great dreams, his determination to cultivate his garden, may be chastised as a philosophy for cozy, merely domestic ethics. But Auden is quite explicit in his belief that on these grounds, and on these grounds only, can meaningful culture—and moreover, the kind of culture which both safeguards us from as a culture being "driven mad" in the way the Germans were and minimizes the danger of becoming like the Nazis in fighting them—be achieved. It is, of course, precisely this view that has caused so many critics to scorn the "new" Auden and long for the earlier, politically-committed Auden. Randall Jarrell, for instance, in a famous attack upon Auden in a 1945 issue of the *Partisan Review*, sneers at "that overweening humility which is the badge of all his saints" and condemns Auden for "moral imbecility" in seeking the salvation of his own soul while heedless of the world being destroyed around him. Jarrell feels that Auden should have somehow put his intellectual powers to work in the war against Hitler rather than criticizing, as Auden did in a 1944 review of a new edition of Grimm's *Märchen*, "the Society for Scientific Diet, the Association of Positivist Parents, the League for the Promotion of Worthwhile Leisure, the Coöperative Camp for Prudent Progressives and all other bores and scoundrels."[5] To which Jarrell: "In the year 1944 these prudent, progressive, scientific, coöperative 'bores and scoundrels' were the enemies with whom Auden found it necessary to struggle. Were *these* your enemies, reader? They were not mine" ("Freud" 187).

Auden did not respond to Jarrell's attack; he rarely if ever responded to attacks, as I have noted in chapter 3. But the attack was in point of fact unfair, and—though the literary critic does not want to sound like counsel for the defense—it is important in this context to explain what was unfair about it. First of all, the precise nature of Jarrell's accusation needs to be made clear. At times Jarrell almost seems to chastise Auden for having failed to enlist as a soldier and to fight in the most literal sense against Hitler's armies. But if such had been his charge, he would have complained that Auden was writing *at all*, rather than complaining about the specific content of his writing. (And Jarrell could not make a general attack on writing in wartime without standing condemned by his own judgment.)

Rather, the essential charge Jarrell levels against Auden is *frivolity*: the allegation is that Auden fiddles while Europe burns. The cause of this frivolity, or rather its justification, according to Jarrell, is Auden's belief in the Christian doctrine (traditionally, if not accurately, identified with Calvinism) of human depravity: because Auden believes that *all* have sinned and fallen short of the glory of God, he has ceased to make moral discriminations, and this is inexcusably frivolous—especially in the midst of this war when moral distinctions between the monstrous Hitler and his opponents are vital.[6]

Were this an accurate representation of Auden's views, he might well be guilty of "moral imbecility." But Auden time and again, in public and in private, expressed his opposition to Hitler and Hitler's cause: for instance, in 1941, in Klaus Mann's magazine *Decision*, he wrote that "the defeat of Hitler is an immediate necessity about which there can be no discussion" (quoted in Carpenter 309). However, he did not believe that in so doing he had exhausted his moral responsibilities, because he did not assume that a given society has all honor and virtue thrust upon it merely through being attacked by an evil force. Auden never, even for an instant, questions whether the force that has attacked the Allies and Western civilization itself is evil; rather, he asks us to be watchful lest (possessed by a "grand apocalyptic dream" of revenge) we become infected with that same evil ourselves. What the doctrine of human depravity does for Auden is simply and constantly to remind him that no one can *assume* himself or herself to be invulnerable to the forces that led, first to the Nazis' supremacy in

Germany itself, and later to the Nazis' determination to conquer all Europe. Jarrell, on the other hand, appears unaware that the war offers to him, or to any loyal citizen of the Allied nations, any moral temptations whatsoever. This is especially odd when one considers Jarrell's poems about the life of a common dogface, which indicate his comprehension of the evil that can be done at least by the leaders of an army, even when that army fights in a just cause.

Moreover, Jarrell does not just misrepresent Auden's understanding of evil and its manifestations in the current war; he also simply misses the essential point of those writings of Auden's that most offend him. The key issue for Auden is not what the ordinary citizen can and should do in the war, but rather what responsibilities the artist, in particular the poet, must carry out. It is clear that Jarrell believes that poets should in some way turn their talents to the fight against Hitler; but he does not, or cannot, explain just how this could be done. In translation or propaganda? In poems about the war? It appears that Jarrell has not considered Auden's striking claim that there is *nothing* a poet, qua poet, can do to fight against Hitler. "[P]oetry makes nothing happen," he famously says (CP 248); moreover,

> art is a product of history, not a cause. Unlike some other products, technical inventions for example, it does not re-enter history as an effective agent, so that the question whether art should or should not be propaganda is unreal. The case for the prosecution [of Yeats, for whom Auden is here imagining himself to be a legal advocate] rests on the fallacious belief that art ever makes anything happen, whereas the honest truth . . . is that, if not a poem had been written, not a picture painted, not a bar of music composed, the history of man would remain materially unchanged. (EA 393)

If Auden is wrong in this belief, he is honestly wrong; and even the most cursory review of the history of Europe will show that the burden of proof rests on those who disagree. It is understandable that Jarrell would *want* to believe that art has the power to change the world, and thus that the writer qua writer can be a significant weapon against "the evil incarnated in Hitler" (a phrase Auden used in conversation with

Golo Mann [Spender, *Tribute* 102]; but it is less understandable that he would exercise such virulence and scorn against a fellow poet who happens to disagree with that assessment of art's power.

However, it would certainly be legitimate for Jarrell to ask why Auden writes at all, given his skepticism about the power of art. Because while poets are not and can never be the unacknowledged legislators of the world—that job, Auden liked to say, better suits the secret police or the Gestapo (see, e.g., DH 27, "Squares" 27)—they can serve their own community by calling certain important but easily neglected facts to remembrance and by warning against some equally easily neglected dangers. Poets cannot fight against Hitler, but they can fight against the people and the tendencies in their own society which corrupt that society from within and on the foundational levels of family and locality. Moreover, it is not inconceivable that some of these corrupting forces are precisely those—"the Society for Scientific Diet, the Association of Positivist Parents, the League for the Promotion of Worthwhile Leisure, the Coöperative Camp for Prudent Progressives" —whom Jarrell explicitly claims *not* to oppose. It is evident, then, that while there is conflict between Jarrell and Auden it does not take the form that Jarrell claims it does: it is not Jarrell's concern for the world versus Auden's concern for his own personal salvation; rather, it is disagreement over *which* enemies may profitably be fought, *which* superindividual concerns the poet may effectively engage in.

Two conclusions, then, emerge from this correction of Jarrell. First, that if Auden sinned, it was only against Jarrell's high view of art, and not against English or American society or against the Allied war effort. And second, a poet who goes out of his way, and against the current cultural grain, to warn of the moral dangers that his society faces as it struggles with a fierce and hateful enemy is guilty of anything but "moral imbecility," anything but frivolity. It is worthwhile to reflect on the social history that made a man as intelligent as Randall Jarrell incapable of recognizing the particular form Auden's seriousness took; for that same social history makes Auden's pursuit of local understanding scandalous and offensive.

What we have done so far, then: first, to trace the history of Auden's conviction that significant culture is and must necessarily be local rather than universal and, second, to defend this conviction against certain misunderstandings, especially those which conceive it to involve a quietistic or even fatalistic withdrawal from all forms of superindividual concern. But what also emerges from reflection on this period of Auden's career is his equally important conviction that this local culture must be deliberately and personally *chosen*. Now, normally those who emphasize the inevitable chosenness of culture (for example, T. S. Eliot) tend also to emphasize its universality, while many communitarian devotees of local culture (for example, Wendell Berry) tend to avoid the question of choice. It is Auden's combination of these two positions that makes him particularly noteworthy.

Let us look at Auden contrasted with the two representative figures just mentioned. Eliot writes, in a famous passage from "Tradition and the Individual Talent," that tradition "cannot be inherited, and if you want it you must obtain it by great labour" (*Selected* 4). Presumably, in light of other things he was writing at the time, Eliot means us to understand that this need to obtain tradition only through heroic effort and deliberate choice is the peculiar curse of the modern age; certainly it would not have afflicted John Donne, who (or so Eliot thought at the time) could "feel [his] thought as immediately as the odour of a rose" (247), living as he did in an age of unified sensibility. It is incidentally important to understand Eliot's later career, his claim to classicism, traditionalism, and so on, to see these positions as choices rather than inherited givens. Recall again the words of Robert Langbaum cited in chapter 2: "Are not, after all, even our new classicisms and new Christian dogmatisms really romanticisms in an age which simply cannot supply the world-views such doctrines depend on, so that they become, for all their claims to objectivity, merely another opinion, the objectification of someone's personal view?" (28). Eliot may not have fully understood the implications of this point, but Auden did. The dialectic of choice and necessity is, as many critics have pointed out, an obsession of Auden's throughout his career, but it is summed up with exemplary clarity in the prayer than concludes "In Sickness and In Health," written just a few months after "New Year Letter": "O hold us to the voluntary way" (SP 115).[7]

But in any case, what most clearly distinguishes Auden from Eliot is the fact that Eliot's chosen tradition is universal and objective: the "ideal order" of *all* great works of art, the forerunner of Northrop Frye's archetypically organized "imaginative universe." It by definition cannot be confined to a place; it repudiates the insular and parochial— opprobrious terms which in its dialect are synonymous with the local. But as we have already seen, for Auden it is precisely the limited particularity of the gathering at Elizabeth Mayer's home that enables those people to come together as a genuine, if tiny, *civitas*. Auden would never write a book, as Eliot did, on *The Idea of a Christian Society*.

Auden may equally well be contrasted with Berry, who relentlessly and eloquently has argued for the beauty of the local and its necessity as a foundation for significant culture. But Berry's consistent emphasis is on the need to conserve and protect existing communities or to restore those that have fallen into neglect and disrepair; he always assumes a history of relations which, if they are not currently active, can be reestablished. Repeatedly in his essays Berry posits *memory* as a necessary component of healthy community. In Berry's scheme, it appears, Auden's first move toward community would have to be a return to England; yet England is the one place where, Auden believed, he could not find genuine community, in part because there was no place in England which he could think of as home, but also and more importantly because the English intelligentsia rejected and scorned the convictions he had come to find essential. (In 1940 Auden told Golo Mann, "The English intellectuals who now cry out to Heaven against the evil incarnated in Hitler have no Heaven to cry to; they have nothing to offer and their protests echo in empty space" [Spender, *Tribute* 102].) Berry cannot, or does not, explain how Auden might find significant local community in America, in New York City of all unlikely places. It is the creation of new community that Auden is concerned with—as he often tried to explain in letters of this period to his puzzled English friends—not the restoration of the old;

and thus the question of choice, which Berry neglects but which is formulated so eloquently by Langbaum in the passage quoted above, is paramount for him.

From the preceding paragraph it becomes evident that, while Berry and Auden alike are proponents of local culture, "local" does not mean the same thing to both. There are common points: local culture as both men use the term is restricted in scope, humble in its aspirations, dedicated to preservation and conservation; moreover, it emphasizes and celebrates the social and communal formation of all personal identities. But for Berry healthy local culture must necessarily be rooted in a particular physical environment, a *place*. Auden does not seem to think so. For more than twenty-five years he lived in New York City, but for only half the year; the other half being spent first on the tiny Italian island of Ischia, later in his beloved home in the village of Kirchstetten in Austria. Auden thought often and wrote beautifully about these localities but clearly felt the need, as Berry perhaps does not, to maintain his community in no place but his own mind and work. The nature of his profession—it is vital to remember that Berry is a farmer as well as a poet and would necessarily have a very different understanding of community and local culture if he only wrote poetry—and of his apparently rootless way of life forced Auden to confront a difficult fact: if he were to experience the blessings of communal, local culture at all, he would have to find a means to cultivate such experience that would seem quite alien to more traditional local cultures.[8] Oddly enough, Auden finds himself in a situation quite similar to that of many of Dostoevsky's characters. Mikhail Bakhtin has described this condition so vividly that his account deserves to be quoted even in this very different context:

> To create a human community in the world, to join several people together outside the framework of available social forms, is the goal of Myshkin, of Alyosha, and in a less conscious and clear-cut form of all Dostoevsky's other heroes. . . . Communion has been deprived, as it were, of its real-life body and wants to create one arbitrarily, out of purely human material. All this is a most profound expression of the social disorientation of the classless intelligentsia, which feels itself

dispersed throughout the world and whose members must orient themselves in the world one by one, alone and at their own risk.

(*Problems* 280–81)

The aptness of this passage for Auden in the early forties is almost eerie: we can see here the need many intellectuals feel for the "organic" rootedness that Gramsci describes, coupled with their sense that they must provide not only their own roots but the soil in which it may grow. Nothing, to Dostoevsky's heroes or to Auden, is simply given.

This "need for roots," as Simone Weil famously called it, explains why Berry's emphasis on memory does eventually come to be essential even to Auden's peculiar form of local culture: Auden does not have the luxury of beginning with a substantial history, but he soon develops one. From about 1940 on Auden very consciously builds a community of friends and colleagues that he sustains and memorializes through his poetry. No other major poet dedicates so many poems to his friends; the reader of Auden's correspondence, especially letters from the last twenty years of his life, finds that he spent an extraordinary amount of time typing up drafts of his poems for friends and asking them if he could dedicate those poems to them. And often the themes of these poems involve Auden's reflections on the very issues of this chapter: under what conditions communities can thrive, what dangers (internal or external) threaten those communities, and, especially, the importance of being continually thankful for the blessings of friendship and "local understanding." Thus a chief purpose of Auden's later poetry becomes the making of a permanent record of the nature and history of his friendships, that is to say, his community. Poetry—for Auden and, he hopes, for his friends—resumes an ancient, lost (and by Auden much-lamented) function, as a mnemonic device. What must be remembered through poetry, however, is not the number of days in April, but rather the character of one's friendships and the virtues of one's community. Like the Jesuit missionary Matteo Ricci (described by the historian Jonathan Spence), Auden builds a memory palace, but this one does not remain a Prosperian "insubstantial pageant": it is inscribed on solid paper and bound between hard covers.

Earlier I mentioned, briefly, "Memorial for the City" as a poem in which Auden repudiates the Constantinian project. But the very title suggests that Auden retains as part of his conceptual framework the notion of a political entity larger than the tiny *civitas* made up of his friends and colleagues. Every local culture, Auden frequently implies, though it is a *polis* unto itself, also participates in that larger entity more usually called the *polis*. It does not often participate well and meaningfully, largely because it remains unconscious of its responsibilities to the greater City, but in the ideal commonwealth the smallest and largest polities will understand their relation: as he writes near the end of "New Year Letter," "The largest *publicum*'s a *res*, / And the least *res* a *publicum*" (CP 240).

One practical consequence of this view is that each local community must recognize the validity of other such communities and accept that each has a place in the fabric of the whole, Berkeley and Orange County alike. Thus the two enemies of "Vespers," the Arcadian and the Utopian, are in fact equally necessary members of what was earlier called their City, but which Auden also, and tellingly, calls "our dear old bag of a democracy" (CP 639).

The challenge that Auden presents, then, is to maintain simultaneous allegiances to one's local culture and to the greater polity—assuming that that polity is a democracy because only in democracy (thinks Auden) can such exceedingly varied and even contradictory local communities be formed and sustained.[9] But it is extraordinarily difficult, even in times such as ours in which there is (supposedly) no higher virtue than toleration, to acknowledge and even celebrate the role one's political opponents play in the constitution of the society. And sad to say, as Auden got older the vision of this great twilit meeting receded and was replaced by withdrawal into the most local of all cultures, the garden cultivated *only* in the mind.

Again, Auden's lack of attachment to a place causes him to think of the formation of community in terms of thankfulness, remembrance, and inscription: to write poems to and for his friends is to remember and give thanks for their friendship, to build a community on the page that cannot, thanks to the international character of Auden's life and his connections, be built in a single location. But however necessary this form of community building was for Auden, he pursued it with such vigor and determination that it gradually assumed a kind of perverse life of its own, so that the local culture that he conceived in his mind and memory became preferable to any more material kind. This tendency he was perfectly aware of, though it is not easy to tell if he regretted it. For instance, in "Thanksgiving for a Habitat" (written mostly from 1962 to 1964), Auden writes that one of the greatest blessings of his Austrian home, a dwelling-place "I dared not hope or fight for," is that there "I needn't, ever, be at home *to /* those I am not at home *with*" (CP 690–91), which is, I suppose, understandable; but he adds these curious lines in the third poem of the sequence, "The Cave of Making," to his recently deceased friend Louis MacNeice:

> I wish you hadn't
> caught that cold, but the dead we miss are easier
>   to talk to: with those no longer
> tensed by problems one cannot feel shy and, anyway,
>   when playing cards or drinking
> or pulling faces are out of the question, what else is there
>   to do but talk to the voices
> of conscience they have become? From now on, as a visitor
>   who needn't be met at the station,
> your influence is welcome at any hour in my ubity. . . .   (692)

MacNeice's ghost might well be pleased at being named a "voice of conscience," but perhaps a little uneasy at being considered a more welcome friend now that Auden doesn't have to go to the trouble of meeting his train, or feeding him and finding him a bed. It is true that the dead, as friends, cause remarkably little trouble, but even to hint that this makes them *better* friends is to betray an unhealthy pleasure in keeping the garden of one's daily routine well tended and undisturbed.[10]

Such a tendency provokes a disturbing question: is something like this fate inevitable for forms of local culture that are not, as Berry would have them be, rooted in a particular place? Is the project of building local culture in poems of recognition and gratitude an impossible one? "The houses of our City," Auden writes in another poem from "Habitat," "Grub First, Then Ethics,"

> are real enough but they lie
> haphazardly scattered over the earth,
>   and Her vagabond forum
> is any space where two of us happen to meet
>   who can spot a citizen
> without papers.   (CP 706)

But is this good enough? Can a *polis* worthy of the name be sustained by occasional meetings of cognoscenti and equally occasional poems from one cognoscente to others? (Bakhtin again: "the classless intelligentsia, which feels itself dispersed throughout the world and whose members must orient themselves in the world one by one, alone and at their own risk.") It seems that Auden feared just that, since the poem goes on,

>   So, too, can Her foes. Where the
>   power lies remains to be seen,
> the force, though, is clearly with them: perhaps only
>   by falling can She become
> Her own Vision, but we have sworn under four eyes
>   to keep Her up. . . .   (706)

This is a curious passage, because it suggests that Auden's attitude toward the local culture he had striven to build closely resembles his attitude toward the poetic art to which he had dedicated his working life. To Louis MacNeice's ghost he writes, "Speech can at best, a shadow echoing / the silent light, bear witness / to the truth it is not" (CP 693), but this is an old idea with him. From "New Year Letter":

> Yet truth, like love and sleep, resents
> Approaches that are too intense,
> And often when the searcher stood
> Before the Oracle, it would
> Ignore his grown-up earnestness
> But not the child of his distress,

> For through the Janus of a joke
> The candid psychopompos spoke.   (CP 206)

This idea finds its fullest development, as we saw in chapter 2, in *The Sea and the Mirror,* where Caliban elaborates his vision of utter aesthetic ineptitude, in which the provincial opera company is so appalled by its own badness that it becomes, for the first time, capable of genuinely recognizing the ideal toward which it has so unsuccessfully striven.

In "Thanksgiving for a Habitat" Auden makes a similar point about the City of which he is a voluntary and self-selected citizen: "perhaps only / by falling can She become / Her own vision" (CP 706). A chief purpose, then, of all humanly built cultures is to produce recognition of the gaping chasm that separates our earthly cities from the City of God, all earthly communities from the communion of the saints. The failures of such cultures, then, are not only to be expected but to be welcomed—but only if the effort to perfect them (or at least "keep them up") has been genuine. As Simone Weil never tired of saying, you can confront your weakness only if you have reached the actual limit of your abilities; failures due to laziness have no educational value (*Waiting* 109).

Is this a perverse and fatalistic conclusion? Or, to the contrary, an unrealistically hopeful one? For the reader who can share Auden's belief in an eternal City of God, his message is chastening but ultimately reassuring: "All will be judged," he says in "At the Grave of Henry James," but in the (later excised) final stanza of that poem he also finds comfort in those words from the Prayer Book about "Him whose property is always to have mercy, the author / And giver of all good things" (SP 123). For the reader who cannot share that faith, Auden may seem to rest too comfortably in his own inevitable failure to sustain any ideal order, however restricted in its scope and aims. But for members of both parties Auden has demonstrated with peculiar poetic clarity just how complex a project the formation of community is and just how difficult are the virtues required to keep it alive and well.

CHAPTER 5

Eros and Agape

By all means sing of love but, if you do,
Please make a rare old proper hullabaloo:
When ladies ask How much do you love me?
The Christian answer is cosí-cosí;
But poets are not celibate divines:
Had Dante said so, who would read his lines?

•   •   •

What but tall tales, the luck of verbal playing,
Can trick [Man's] lying nature into saying
That love, or truth in any serious sense,
Like orthodoxy, is a reticence?
                    —"'THE TRUEST POETRY IS THE MOST FEIGNING'"

Some of Auden's commentators have written extensively and sympathetically about the Christian elements in his later work, while maintaining a discreet silence about the embarrassing matter of his homosexuality. Other, more recent critics have written extensively and sympathetically about his homosexuality, while maintaining a discreet silence about the embarrassing matter of his Christian faith. Each tendency is to be deplored, especially if one wishes to understand

Auden's thinking about love—and there is little about which he thought more often. It is not merely coincidental that two of the most momentous events in Auden's life, his falling in love with Chester Kallman and his returning to Christianity, occurred little more than a year apart. Throughout the rest of Auden's life, his thoughts about erotic love and about the love of God would remain interwoven or, perhaps, entangled—so much so that it is impossible to intelligently discuss the one without invoking the other. There is no subject about which Auden thought so constantly, so intelligently, and, in the end, so confusingly.

Edward Mendelson rightly says that "Auden's early poems are for intense love affairs that end quickly; the later poems are for marriage" (*Early* 22).[1] Love for the early Auden is desire, flared up and burning— or, in a metaphor he employed while in a more academic mood, an extensive series of "new glosses on the noun Amor" ("Letter to Lord Byron" [CP 110]). Inconstancy, like that traditionally associated with the moon, and immediacy are the givens of this erotic world:

> This lunar beauty
> Has no history,
> Is complete and early;
> If beauty later
> Bear any feature
> It had a lover
> And is another.   (CP 55)

These twin themes are best exemplified in the most famous and brilliant of Auden's love poems, "Lay your sleeping head, my love" (CP 157–58). In this poem's world, though "the grave / Proves the child ephemeral," for the moment that loved one is "entirely beautiful." That "Certainty, fidelity / On the stroke of midnight pass," that "Beauty, midnight, vision" all evaporate are facts enunciated but not regretted. The poem ends not with the speaker's promise to continue loving, but with a farewell wish that this "child" will continue to be loved by all whom he or she encounters: "Nights of insult let you pass / Watched by every human love."

Professions of lasting love are at this point in Auden's career (and later, too) the object of satire and moral reproof. One thinks especially of the metaphorically extravagant lover of "As I Walked Out One Evening," whose promise of fidelity is mocked by the disenchanting voices of the city's clocks: "'O let not Time deceive you, / You cannot conquer Time'" (CP 134). A more sober speaker, in an untitled song, not only predicts that Death will bring an end to "Beauty's conquest of [his lover's] face," but also calmly assures his beloved that his current vows will break before Death comes (137).

A decade later, in "In Praise of Limestone," the inconstancy of love and the ephemerality of beauty are again matters of concern, but now the concern is moral, and cogitation upon them troubles the waters of the spirit. This poem begins by speaking of "we, the inconstant ones" and ends with a reference to "the blessed, [who] will not care what angle they are regarded from, / Having nothing to hide," but it would be a mistake to see these two groups as mutually exclusive or even contrastive—even though the poem is in some ways a confession of moral vacillation.[2] I make this emphasis in light of the central text that stands behind "In Praise of Limestone," the third canto of Dante's *Paradiso,* featuring the nun Piccarda, who represents those who were inconstant in their love of God. Piccarda's inconstancy on earth did not damn her; she remains forever among the blessed, and as such receives as much grace as God can give her; but what she is capable of receiving is, in eternity, limited by the choices she made on earth. She will forever be a vessel less capacious than the great saints; her sphere, of course, is that of the moon.[3] "In Praise of Limestone" is, above all else, Auden's recognition that he and Piccarda are spiritually kin. What is expressed here is not the fear of damnation, but regret that inconstancy limits one's capacity even to imagine, let alone to achieve, the purity of heart which, as Kierkegaard famously said, is to will one thing. The concluding lines of the poem must be read in light of these considerations:

> In so far as we have to look forward
> To death as a fact, no doubt we are right: But if
> Sins can be forgiven, if bodies rise from the dead,

> These modifications of matter into
> Innocent athletes and gesticulating fountains,
>   Made solely for pleasure, make a further point:
> The blessed will not care what angle they are regarded from,
>   Having nothing to hide. Dear, I know nothing of
> Either, but when I try to imagine a faultless love
>   Or the life to come, what I hear is the murmur
> Of underground streams, what I see is a limestone landscape.   (CP 542)

It is essential to note that Auden's poem praises, not the inconstancy that limestone represents for him, but rather the limestone itself as a reminder that his inconstancy limits what he can know or even imagine. The difference is enormously important. Auden does not deny that he will become one of "the blessed" or that he will then have "nothing to hide." But if and when that does happen, it will be the result of an unmerited divine gift and because inconstancy, like all other sins, "can be forgiven." The blessed are both like and unlike the "nude young male" from early in the first published version of the poem, who "lounges / Against a rock displaying his dildo" (SP 185). He too has nothing to hide, he too knows "that for all his faults he is loved"; but he places his whole confidence in his "power to charm," whereas the blessed trust the one whom Auden once called (in "At the Grave of Henry James") "the author / And giver of all good things" (SP 123).

As in some earlier chapters, I am concerned here with investigating how Auden got from the one point to the other—from the celebration of transitoriness in "Lay your sleeping head, my love" to the regretful acceptance of inconstancy in "In Praise of Limestone"—and also if possible to isolate a pivotal moment at which the exchange of one tradition, or set of assumptions, for another becomes operative in his work. In this case the pivotal moment seems clear: the 1940 poem "In Sickness and in Health" (especially in its original form, as preserved in Mendelson's edition of the *Selected Poems*). And what an exploration of this poem will reveal, among other things, is the first direct evidence in Auden's work of the aforementioned entanglement of eros and agape.

The poem begins, like a penitential liturgy, with a confession of sin:

Dear, all benevolence of fingering lips
That does not ask forgiveness is a noise
    At drunken feasts where Sorrow strips
To serve some glittering generalities. . . .   (SP 111)

The sin confessed here is, of course, the writing of a love poem. The phrasing bears the marks of Auden's later penchant for what Lucy McDiarmid calls the *retractio*, except that it still holds out hope that poetic music (the "benevolence of fingering lips") may be at least partly redeemed by a preliminary confession of its own inability to achieve the specificity and exclusivity of meaning that Auden thinks appropriate to poems about those one loves, whether human or divine. (This is a point to which we will have to return.) But to begin a love poem in this way is to cast a shadow not only on the verbal expression of love but on the love itself. And indeed the first half or more of the poem is an extended description of the agonies of love, with an accompanying warning against the making of lovers' vows which echoes and reverses that line so linked with weddings, "O promise me":

O promise nothing, nothing, till you know
The kingdom offered by the love-lorn eyes
A land of condors, sick cattle, and dead flies. . . .

O let none say I Love until aware
What huge resources it will take to nurse
    One ruining speck, one tiny hair
That casts a shadow through the universe. . . .   (111–12)

Then, as he would later describe the two Hells of Romanticism in *The Sea and the Mirror*, he here describes two dominant, yet opposing, simulacra of genuine love, simulacra which, through their power as models in Western culture, have brought generations of would-be lovers to moral ruin.[4] On the one hand we have Tristan and Isolde, whose idealized vision of love causes them to prefer death to the quotidian mundanity which inevitably accompanies actual sexual intercourse. Therefore, they,

Deliciously postponing their delight,
Prolong frustration till it lasts all night,
Then perish lest Brangaene's worldly cry
Should sober their cerebral ecstasy.   (112)

Their counter-archetype is Don Juan, who fears death above all things
and can lose that fear only in an endless series of trysts. Don Juan, the
most famous of all seducers of women, is used here by Auden to
depict an aging predatory gay male, searching always for boys: "angels
to keep him chaste," that is, free from the passion for death that he
sees in Tristan and Isolde:

a helpless, blind
unhappy spook, he haunts the urinals,
Existing solely by their miracles.   (112)

Gregory Woods says that Auden is "not uncritical" of these archetypes
(146), which seems to me an understatement so drastic that it becomes
a misunderstanding. Elsewhere Auden calls them "diseases of the
Christian imagination" and claims that "their influence upon human
conduct, particularly in their frivolous watered-down modern versions, which gloss over the fact that both the romantic couple and the
solitary seducer are intensely unhappy, has been almost wholly bad"
(F&A 25). Tristan-Isolde and Don Juan are the twin pitfalls of eros,
the lovers' Scylla and Charybdis. Proper meditation on them produces
this recognition, the culmination of the poem's penitential first part:

Beloved, we are always in the wrong,
Handling so clumsily our stupid lives,
   Suffering too little or too long,
Too careful even in our selfish loves....   (113)

Echoed here is Kierkegaard's famous claim that in relation to God we
are always in the wrong (*Either/Or* 595); but the poem pointedly does
not mention a party in relation to whom our wrongness consists. It
is hard, while reading "In Sickness and In Health," not to think of
Auden's near-mad jealousy when he learned (not more than a few
months before writing the poem) that Chester Kallman was not and

never intended to be sexually or romantically faithful to him—a jealousy which promoted Auden to thoughts of murder.[5] In that context the phrase "we are always in the wrong" seems an invitation to mutual confession—I'll admit that I've wronged you if you admit that you've wronged me—as a preliminary to placing their relationship on the moral and spiritual footing which Auden now thought appropriate to a marriage. And he did understand himself as married to Kallman: not long after falling in love Auden had begun wearing a wedding ring (Carpenter 262), and he refers to that object obliquely in an apostrophic prayer—concerned with Tristan and Isolde's love-religion, now virtually named as idolatrous—whose addressee has now become, and will remain through the rest of the poem, God; that is, Love Itself rather than the beloved:

> O, lest we manufacture in our flesh
> The lie of our divinity afresh,
> Describe round our chaotic malice now,
> The arbitrary circle of a vow.   (113)

It does not seem likely that Auden, through this poem or through other means, convinced Kallman to participate with him in this rite, this newly moralized understanding of genuine eros. When Auden referred to an extended trip he and Kallman took to the American West as their "honeymoon," Chester merely commented to a friend, "*Such* a romantic girl" (Davenport-Hines 194).

The lines just quoted are in keeping with the penitential tone of the first part of the poem, but in fact they come in the second part, whose general mood is set by the word which ends the eighth stanza and begins the ninth: "Rejoice." Again the liturgical model is appropriate: in the Anglican tradition, immediately after the General Confession of sin comes the celebration of the Eucharist, in which divisions are reconciled and sufferings healed. And what Auden rejoices most greatly in, and is most thankful to God for, is Chester Kallman. In that ninth stanza (marked as transitional by its being printed in italics) Auden invokes, again somewhat obliquely, God's act of speaking to the suffering Job out of the whirlwind:

Who showed the whirlwind how to be an arm,
And gardened from the wilderness of space
The sensual properties of one dear face? (113)

Auden is on something of a tightrope here: his love for Chester is not something to be seized in the predatory manner of Don Juan, but also not to be deified after the example of Tristan and Isolde; instead it is a gift from God. To remain balanced on this tightrope requires, among other things, a relentless emphasis on the materiality of eros ("the *sensual* properties of one dear face") and a refusal to engage in a Manichean or Gnostic elevation of love into some putative spiritual realm where it can claim perfect purity:

That reason may not force us to commit
That sin of the high-minded, sublimation,
    Which damns our soul by praising it,
Force our desire, O Essence of creation,
To seek Thee always in Thy substances,
Till the performance of those offices
Our bodies, Thine opaque enigmas, do,
Configure Thy transparent justice too.   (114)

Here is a key: God's justice is transparent, but in our bodies (and while on earth we love only in and with our bodies[6]) we may only "configure" it opaquely and enigmatically. Just as in *The Sea and the Mirror* we learn that a stumbling and incompetent mimicry of divine truth is the best any artist can do, so here we learn that lovers can see one another, as well as the God who is Love, only through a glass darkly. And this, Auden believes, is as it should be and indeed prays for reminders that his love is indeed a fallen thing in a fallen world:

                lest we
Mock virtue with its pious parody
And take our love for granted, Love, permit
Temptations always to endanger it. . . .

That we, though lovers, may love soberly,
O Fate, O *Felix Osculum*, to us
Remain nocturnal and mysterious. . . .   (114–15)

By a typically Kierkegaardian paradox, only a love which reminds itself constantly of its own essential shabbiness and ineptitude can hope to honor the God whose gift it is. Divine love does not invite competition. What must be avoided—to stick with the Kierkegaardian terms that are essential here—is the *ethical* justification of erotic love. If the aesthetic realm knows itself to be aesthetic and understands its failure to achieve the fullness of meaning which can only be achieved in and by the religious sphere, then—as Kierkegaard wrote in his *Journals*, the one-volume Oxford edition of which was probably the most important single book for the Auden of this period—then "the aesthetic relation appears again, though paradoxically, as higher than the ethical" (#887).

This element of Auden's thinking about love has not been well understood, and that misunderstanding has led to further misunderstandings of Auden's feelings about his homosexuality. Critics have too readily accepted Christopher Isherwood's verdict, made to seem more authoritative by the quietly perfect sentence in which it is expressed: "His religion condemned it and he agreed that it was sinful, though he fully intended to go on sinning" (*Christopher* 249). It is true that Auden, by the time he wrote "In Sickness and In Health," had long since given up hope of being "cured" of his sexual orientation— Gregory Woods persuasively argues that the 1932 poem "The chimneys are smoking" (EA 116–18) constitutes a "dismissal of the myth of a cure for homosexuality" (146)—but he continued to think of it as a perversion, a swerving from normalcy caused probably by his relationship with his mother.[7] Yet this "perversion" was also in a strange way a blessing from God to him because it helped to preserve him from the idolatry of erotic love that he might have been subject to had he been heterosexual.[8]

This unusual attitude toward erotic love also helps Auden reconcile his personal experience with the theological positions he tended to take in his first years as an adult Christian. Those positions could generally be described—Auden so described them in a 1943 letter— as "Neo-Calvinist (i.e. Barthian)" (Carpenter 301). It is not surprising that a man who was led toward Christian faith by reading Kierkegaard would be drawn to Barth's theology, for both thinkers share an emphasis on the transcendence of God. God for both Barth and Kierkegaard is, in Barth's famous phrase, *Ganz Andere*; He is the God who says, "my thoughts are not your thoughts, nor are your ways my ways" (Isaiah 55:8). Such thinking is no idiosyncrasy which Barth and Kierkagaard happen to share; rather, it is characteristically—one might say fundamentally—Lutheran and has its roots in Luther's rejection of the Catholic tradition of natural theology.[9] That rejection has enormous implications for any theology of love—especially Auden's, as we shall see.

Had Auden been a Roman Catholic, or even a Protestant sympathetic to the traditions of natural theology, the making of a connection between his Christian faith and his relationship with Chester Kallman would have been far less problematic. For he would have had ready to hand a useful intellectual tool, the old (originally Platonic) notion of the *scala amoris*. The natural theology tradition—whose Biblical roots are no less deep, though they are different, than those of the Lutheran tradition (see especially Romans 1:20)—teaches that we may come to know God through coming to know anything and everything that God has made. All things, having been created by God, reveal something of their creator, even if that revelation has been obscured by human sinfulness. Therefore human love may be seen as mirroring, in however imperfect a way, the love of God, and to that degree is a good. However, it ceases to be a good when it is valued for its own sake as the highest good and ceases to lead us toward the higher love of God. One cannot allow oneself to remain on the lower rungs of the ladder without risking damnation—and indeed, Auden once noted, no one who has a genuine glimpse of the Divine in erotic love can ever again be satisfied with the merely erotic (F&A 65).

This tradition Auden knew very well. He had encountered it not only in Plato and in Dante[10]—where, in the poetic description of Beatrice and his history with her, we find one of the fullest and most characteristic developments of its themes—but also in the peculiar writings of Charles Williams, which were instrumental in leading

Auden towards Christian faith. It was through Williams's *The Descent of the Dove* that Auden was introduced to Kierkegaard—an ironic fact, since on the question of natural theology Williams and Kierkegaard are diametrically opposed. For Williams, in developing what he called "romantic theology" (a theology that obsessed Williams, though the reader of *The Descent of the Dove* gets it only in bits and pieces), went far beyond Dante's *scala amoris*: he argued that erotic love is virtually *the* royal road to the knowledge of God (see Cavaliero passim). Thus Auden had available to him, and from sources which he valued greatly, a theology which would justify and even celebrate his love for Chester Kallman as a means of coming closer to God. And early in his Christian life—perhaps significantly, before he learned of Chester's unfaithfulness—while reviewing de Rougemont he would speak of agape as "Eros mutated by grace, a conversion, not an addition, the Law fulfilled, not the Law destroyed" ("Eros" 757), a theme to which he would return from time to time.

Yet from other equally valued sources he was getting a very different message, that agape alone is truly love, all else a series of counterfeits. This, among other things, is the burden of Kierkegaard's *Works of Love*; echoes of it are heard from time to time in his *Journals*. It seems likely that Auden had read, by the early forties, Anders Nygren's *Agape and Eros*, which was then and probably still remains the most comprehensive account of the severest Lutheran division between agape and eros, and its concomitant rejection of the characteristically Catholic concept of caritas.[11] For the Lutheran tradition Bonaventure's famous title, *Itinerarium Mentis In Deum* (the journey of the mind towards God), describes an impossibility: human beings are utterly incapable of moving towards God, by a ladder or any other means. Instead we must focus on the journey the Bible repeatedly describes, which is that of God toward humanity. In this scheme, to which I believe Auden was more and more drawn, though he never fully embraced it, no road leads from the human loves to divine love (by which I mean God's love for us and our fully Christ-like love for our neighbors—the word *agape* typically encompasses both). Instead, God must act, through what Calvinists call "prevenient grace," to transform the lovers and their love. It is telling that by 1949 Auden was, in a letter to Chester, explicitly rejecting the notion that Chester was his Beatrice (Farnan 157), though earlier he had implied just such an identification by saying, in a letter to Chester, that "through you . . . God has chosen to show me my beatitude" (Farnan 65). In the *Vita Nuova*, when the young Dante first sees Beatrice, he hears a voice, "the spirit of the senses which dwells on high," saying "*Apparuit iam beatitudo vestra*" (30) —or, as Auden translates it in an essay, "Now you have seen your beatitude" (F&A 68). This is somewhat ambiguous: in the *Vita Nuova* Beatrice *is* Dante's beatitude (as her name suggests), while Auden describes Chester as *the means by which* he sees his beatitude. This may be a case of keeping eros in its proper place, a place more modest than that which Dante (or Charles Williams) assigned it; and it is probably not coincidental that the letter was written several months *after* Auden had been devastated by learning of Chester's infidelity. Nevertheless, it is significant not only that eight years later Auden rejects the notion of Chester-as-Beatrice but also that he feels that the notion must be openly repudiated. A year after that, if Auden could still speak of agape as the "fulfillment" of eros, he would add that agape is also Eros's "correction"[12]; in 1964 he would write that it must be "transfigured but not annihilated" (F&A 68). In short, if Auden was in his early days with Chester inclined towards a Dantean understanding of eros, that understanding was soon chastened. Even "In Sickness and in Health," which was written before the infidelity and Auden's consequent jealousy, is, as we have seen, remarkably sober in its view of the complications and dangers of erotic love.

(Precisely *how* might eros be fulfilled, corrected, transfigured? On this point Auden is not clear, but in 1948 he suggested that since homoerotic love is not oriented towards familial responsibilities, it "is free to develop in any direction the lovers choose, and that direction should be towards wisdom which, once acquired, will enable them to teach human beings procreated in the normal way how to become a good society. For love is to be judged by its social and political value" [F&A 23]. That last claim seems to me staggering in its implications, but Auden, to my knowledge, never explored them. Nor did he, again to my knowledge, ever explain what it means to say that an erotic relationship can develop in the direction of wisdom.[13])

The great advantage of this chastened view of eros for Auden is that it relieves the enormous pressure placed upon him by the traditional Christian understanding of homosexuality as deviant and perverse. For if all forms of specifically human love are separated from agape by a gulf or chasm (perhaps not as "essential" or "emphatic" as that mentioned by Caliban in his exploration of the aesthetic poverty of his imaginary operatic troupe) then homoerotic love is not in this fundamental respect different from any of eros's other manifestations. The only really important difference is that the moral condemnation placed upon homosexuality by Bible, church, and society curbs the inclination to celebrate homoerotic love as something divine. Thus the homosexual, as noted earlier, is actually in a better position than the heterosexual to recognize that, in relation to God, he or she is in the wrong.

It is difficult to overstress the distance of this view of love from that of the earlier poems, with their celebration of a transient "lunar beauty" and their embrace of faithlessness. What is perhaps most remarkable about this transition is that—to return to the Kierkegaardian terms used earlier—it completely bypasses, or overleaps, the ethical stage in its voyage from the aesthetic to the religious. The one note that is utterly missing from Auden's love poetry, at any stage of his career, is that of Kierkegaard's Judge Wilhelm, whose arguments for the superiority of the ethical to the aesthetic, of marriage to seduction, occupy the second half of *Either/Or*. After all, the ethical is the one stage in which Auden's love for Chester is (in Auden's view) most vulnerable to critique. In a review, published in 1944, of the Swenson-Lowrie translation of *Either/Or*, Auden tries to describe how each of the stages responds to a particular situation, in this case a theft. For the aesthetic realm the fundamental question is how interesting the theft is; for the ethical, whether the theft violates the immutable moral law (which in its view a theft always does). The religious position, though, is more complex:

In treating the theft as an individual act of will which cannot be judged in abstraction from the concrete temporal situation in which it occurs, the Religious sides with the Esthetic against the Ethical in upholding the unique importance of the individual will. But in asserting that the good act—not stealing—is always and only the product of a good will, and the bad act—stealing—always the product of an evil will, it sides with the Ethical against the Esthetic belief that to will is valuable in itself. Lastly, it disagrees with both in blessing an act neither for its manifestly interesting appearance nor for its demonstrably good result, but for its hidden subjective intention. ("Preface" 684)

This description sheds much light on the questions we have been exploring. In the hierarchy of stages that Auden here deploys, the ethical stage's negative judgment on his homosexuality is not annulled —the religious agrees with the ethical that the wrong act stems from a wrong will—but rather superseded by the religious stage's higher concern for the elemental intention which, properly understood, can situate and even transform the ethical judgment. Thus Auden could believe that, even given the sinfulness of homosexual love, his relationship with Chester could be "converted," "transformed," and "corrected" by mutual monandrous commitment, which is why he says, in a campily sardonic letter to Chester, that what "Miss God" demands of him is "a chaste fidelity to the Divine Miss K" (Farnan 158). In this sense and in this sense only Isherwood would be right to say that Auden agreed that his homosexuality was sinful but fully intended to go on sinning.

Such a position could be readily caricatured, since it seems to allow for an extraordinary degree of pure self-justification. But that is not what Auden is up to: he is willing to remain under the ethical judgment that his homosexuality is wrong and to repent appropriately— though never to foreclose on the possibility that God may bring a blessing even to acts that grow from an "evil will."[14] To remain under that judgment without excuse or pretense leads inevitably to suffering, and suffering is the one necessary manifestation of the genuine religious stage. Stephen Spender wrote of the Auden he knew in the 1940s that "as an Anglican, Auden had difficulties to overcome in accepting the moral and ethical judgments of the Church." But there was a marked difference between this Auden and the one Spender had known when they were students and then poets together: "Just as previously he had fitted the world around him into a Freudian or a Marxist pattern, now he fitted it into a Christian one. But now he accepted a dogma which criticized him and which was not simply an instrument for criticizing others" (*World* 271). (Randall Jarrell, having failed to see the judgmental superiority of the earlier Auden—failed largely because it was his own judgmental superiority that he admired when he saw it in another—thought Auden had moved in just the opposite direction: "his morals are now [in 1945], like the law in Luther and Niebuhr, merely a crutch to beat people into submission with" ["Freud" 160].)

There is no doubt that Chester's promiscuity caused Auden great pain and, moreover, that that pain was intensified by the uneasable tension between the Christian ethic and Auden's gayness. But it is remarkable how little he says about this pain, either in his poetry or in the surviving letters. He would not do what he thought Kierkegaard had done, congratulate himself on the spiritual superiority conferred on him by his suffering. His silence on this point testifies to his commitment to a pair of themes which echo and re-echo in his later work: the repeated declaration that "orthodoxy is reticence" (which he sometimes attributed to an unnamed Anglican bishop and sometimes simply to "Anonymous") and the commandment "Bless what there is for being" (CP 591). There are, though, hints of this pain, as we have seen, in "In Sickness and in Health" and a rather full treatment of the experience of jealousy in the words of Joseph in *For the Time Being*. If "In Sickness" and the Christmas letter to Chester suggest that there can be, if only in a mirrorlike and paradoxical way, some relation between eros and agape, the words of Joseph testify to a fear that even such an awkward reconciliation is impossible because there is no divine love to make it possible:

Where are you, Father, where?
Caught in the jealous trap
Of an empty house I hear

As I sit alone in the dark
Everything, everything,
The drip of the bathroom tap,
The creak of the sofa spring,
The wind in the air-shaft, all
Making the same remark
Stupidly, stupidly,
Over and over again.
Father, what have I done?
Answer me, Father, how
Can I answer the tactless wall
Or the pompous furniture now?
Answer them . . .

   . . . .

How then am I to know,
Father, that you are just?
Give me one reason.

   . . . .

All I ask is one
Important and elegant proof
That what my Love had done
Was really at your will
And that your will is Love.   (CP 363–64)

According to Alan Ansen, Auden said flatly, "Joseph is me" (13). (He also told Ansen that the only character in opera he identifies with is King Mark, the cuckold, in *Tristan und Isolde* [92].) The "proof" that erotic tribulation is spiritually meaningful was not forthcoming: to Joseph's plea Gabriel replies, "No you must believe; / Be silent, and sit still" (364), a command which echoes Pascal's famous claim that all the misfortunes of humanity derive from our inability to sit still in a room (Pascal 67). And the narrator's counsel to Joseph implicitly warns him against Kierkegaard's constant reflection on the intensity of his suffering and the extraordinariness of his situation: "To choose what is difficult all one's days / As if it were easy, that is faith. Joseph, praise" (365). Not only is Joseph denied any substantive reason to believe that he is loved by Mary or by God, he is told to avoid overmuch scrutiny of the question. Joseph's only valid response is that of Eliot in "Ash-Wednesday," a poem which lurks behind several sections of *For the Time Being* and which is filled with its own Pascalian echoes, "Teach us to care and not to care / Teach us to sit still" (*Collected* 86).

As we saw in chapter 2, that Auden was sometimes tempted to take up Prospero's mantle, and Prospero understood perfectly well the greatest challenge he would face upon his return to Milan: "Can I learn to suffer / Without saying something ironic or funny / On suffering?" (CP 409). Better, when enduring the agonies of jealousy, to do so silently—"I never suspected," says Prospero in his next sentence, "the way of truth / Was a way of silence"—or at most to speak obliquely and indirectly, through a character in an oratorio.

Indeed, a Kierkegaardian "indirect communication" becomes the model for Auden's treatment of love—eros and agape alike—for most of the rest of his career. (This tendency runs parallel to the penchant for retraction which Lucy McDiarmid has described.) It is not just suffering which cannot, or should not, be represented directly in poetry; the joys of love likewise evade the resources of poetry, as Auden explains in his reflective prose meditation—which, perhaps significantly, he includes in his *Collected Poems* rather than in one of his collections of prose—"Dichtung und Wahrheit (An Unwritten Poem)" (CP 649–63). This set of fifty *pensées*, written in 1959, stands in a curious relation to "Postscript: Christianity and Art," another set of *pensées* which seems to have been written at about the same time. In the latter piece Auden expresses his "uneasiness" with Christian devotional poetry, and explicitly contrasts it to erotic poetry:

> It is quite in order that a poet should write a sonnet expressing his devotion to Miss Smith because the poet, Miss Smith, and all his readers know perfectly well that, had he chanced to fall in love with Miss Jones instead, his feelings would be exactly the same. But if he writes a sonnet expressing his devotion to Christ, the important point, surely, is that his devotion is felt for Christ and not for, say, Buddha or Mahomet, and this point cannot be made in poetry; the Proper Name proves nothing. (DH 458)

Yet in "Dichtung und Wahrheit" Auden has precisely the same qualm about erotic poetry, perhaps because he is now the lover rather than the theoretician:

> It would not be enough that I should believe that what I had written was true: to satisfy me, the truth of this poem must be self-evident. It would have to be written, for example, in such a way that no reader could misread *I love You* as "I love you." (CP 649)

But this is impossible, since "Speech . . . lacks the Indicative Mood. . . ." "All its statements are in the subjunctive and only possibly true until verified (which is not always possible) by non-verbal evidence" (650–51). Or, to put the whole matter aphoristically, "Which is Tristan? Which Don Giovanni? No Peeping Tom can tell" (653). It is not "quite in order" for Tristan that the reader (by analogy a Peeping Tom) cannot tell his love poetry from the seductive verse of Don Giovanni; and therefore Auden's prospective love poem remains "unwritten," even though its absence is noted and meditated upon. If in the "Postscript" erotic and agapic poetry are firmly distinguished, in "Dichtung und Wahrheit" they stand under the same judgment.[15] Silence is best; indirection the only valid alternative.

Auden had always been somewhat uneasy about erotic poetry—only rarely, as in "Lay your sleeping head," did he allow the expression of love to emerge without implicit ironic quotation marks; and even there, the echoes of Yeatsian rhetoric may tempt some readers to ironic interpretation. More typical of the early Auden is "Funeral Blues" (CP 141, where it bears no title), recently made famous by its perfectly serious and deeply moving employment in the film *Four Weddings and a Funeral*. The poem makes available to the reader who so chooses a more distanced and even sardonic tone, as does "O the valley in the summer where I and my John" (142), a poem which Auden coupled with "Funeral Blues" in the selection of his work he made for a Modern Library edition (calling them "Two Songs for Hedli Anderson") and which, like its companion, can be read either as a parody or a profoundly earnest employment of popular song form.

But when Auden fell in love with Chester Kallman and returned to Christianity the stakes were raised for any poetry of love—a fact which the complexity and inconsistency of his thinking on this subject both bear witness to. Clearly, Auden felt drawn to the writing of erotic poetry; "compelled" would not be too strong a word. (Did he feel equally drawn to writing poems about the love of God or of his neighbor? Probably not; but whatever attraction of that kind he may have felt was clearly overcome by his scruples regarding the "Proper Name" and poetry's lack of the "Indicative Mood.") The problem was to find a medium which allowed him to exercise this compulsion without running headlong into the problems delineated in "Dichtung und Wahrheit." This was a problem indeed, and perhaps it is not surprising that erotic poetry recedes from Auden's work in the forties. There are Joseph's song of jealousy in *For the Time Being*, the songs of Ferdinand and Miranda in *The Sea and the Mirror*, but little else. Only in *The Age of Anxiety* (1947) does a serious, if rather theoretical, interest in eros return, and even there it is quickly displaced. For instance, after the "marriage" of Rosetta and Emble, he passes out on her bed, rendering consummation impossible, and her reflections on this event (or nonevent) quickly and curiously swerve into a meditation on the character of her Jewishness. The ironic contextualization of the lover's ecstasy which was a commonplace in Auden's early poetry occasionally returns later on, in the fifties: the dispersuadable Furies await the lovers in "Deftly, admiral, cast your fly" (573), while two listening birds critique another ecstatic *professeur d'amour* in "The starling and a willow-wren" (574–75). But the chief medium for love poetry, in Auden's later career, is clearly the opera.

The chief question about Auden's fascination with the opera is why it did not happen earlier; the likely answer is that it was displaced by his absorption in the theatrical writing he did in the thirties with Isherwood. After an early exposure to at least some music of Wagner, he seems, despite a deep love for music and considerable musical literacy, to have ignored opera altogether until he met Kallman.

Perhaps the emotional extravagance of opera (about which more in a moment) was at first uncongenial to a man who sought so consistently to achieve emotional discipline. Auden attributed his neglect simply to "the musical fashion of [his] youth," for which he was later "eternally grateful" because it prevented him from listening, to Italian opera especially, until he was "capable of appreciating a world so beautiful and so challenging to [his] own cultural heritage" (DH 40).

But in the event, writing opera libretti had the immediate effect of enabling Auden to become the artistic servant he wanted to be: he repeatedly insisted on the subordinate role of the librettist to the composer. "The first duty of the librettist is, needless to say, to write verses which excite the musical imagination of the composer; if these verses should also possess poetic merit in themselves, so much the better, but such merit is a secondary consideration" (L 615). So said Auden and Kallman, upon the American premiere of *The Rake's Progress* in 1953. Auden claimed that the librettist's words "are as expendable as infantry to a Chinese general," a simile he clearly relished, considering the frequency with which he used it (e.g., DH 473, L 611). But he also said, in a letter to Hans-Werner Henze about *The Bassarids*, that he and Kallman wanted their libretto to be *printed* as written, however many cuts and alterations it would ultimately undergo on the road to performance (L 682). Let the Chinese generals do what they may, the mothers of these infantrymen want their children brought back home once the battle is over.

When Auden wrote, as he often did, of his duty to sacrifice his aesthetic preferences to practical utility—recall his need, as a child, to choose ore-washing equipment for an imaginary concentrating mill (discussed in chapter 2)—his problem was not how to eradicate the emotions but rather how to find a proper place for their expression. Writing for the opera solved this problem beautifully, because emotional extravagance is virtually its *raison d'etre*: in this case it was Auden's unequivocal duty to *unleash*, rather than restrain, the emotional resources of poetic language. "A credible situation in an opera means a situation in which it is credible that someone should sing. A good libretto plot . . . offers as many opportunities as possible for the characters to be swept off their feet" (DH 471). Thus the young lovers of the *Elegy for Young Lovers*, Toni and Elizabeth, can and should sing this imitation folk song to a departing friend:

> A stream runs down the valley,
> A mill-wheel spins away,
> It grinds the precious flower
> Of love both night and day.
>
> But now the wheel is broken
> And love is at an end
> And two who walked together
> By different roads will wend.
>
> Give me your hand; who ever
> Believed that we should part,
> Or summer change to winter
> And light to heavy heart?   (L 231)

Can a card-carrying modernist take such a phrase as "the precious flower / Of love" seriously—at least when it appears on the page? In strictly literary terms the whole song could fairly be called lugubrious, in an adolescent sort of way: the last two stanzas in particular are a pure pastiche of Housman, whom Auden thought the great poet of male adolescence (F&A 332). But in the full operatic context, such emotional intensity and apparent overemphasis are proper; anything less would be insufficient. "Opera is the last refuge of the High style" in poetry, Auden wrote (*Secondary Worlds* 102); moreover, if the music is good enough the audience will believe without qualification in the validity of the emotions represented. (Auden once saw, in the same week, a performance of Wagner's *Tristan* and Jean Cocteau's cinematic adaptation of the story, *L'Eternal Retour*. "During the former," he reported, "two souls, weighing over two hundred pounds apiece, were transfigured by a transcendent power; in the latter, a handsome boy met a beautiful girl and they had an affair" [DH 469].) Now, any given opera as a whole need not accept without question the validity of these emotions: "the crowning glory of opera is the big ensemble"

(470) because such an ensemble provides the necessary context for situating each aria or duet, a context which may cause us to question the emotions of certain arias. But each aria or duet, *as it is being sung*, commands our complete assent: as long as Toni and Elizabeth are singing, since "music is immediate, not reflective" and in it "whatever is sung is the case" (471), there is no place for ironic references to callow Housmanesque melancholia. The librettists' words should encourage this assent rather than fight against it: thus the need in opera for a florid and emotionally extravagant style, even if poetry on the page, at least in the modern world, makes room only for "the wry, the sotto-voce, / Ironic and monochrome" (CP 622). As a librettist Auden was more than permitted, he was *obliged*, not to confine or interrogate love and its kindred emotions, but rather cut them loose.

For the poetry of agape, Auden, it seems to me, found no equivalent to the world of opera. The Horatian poetry of friendship (as discussed in chapter 4) perhaps could be said to represent one facet of agape but only if one subsumes philia under agape's canopy. *The Bassarids*, as a religious drama, may be understood as evoking a God of love by emphasizing its absence from the Euripidean text on which the libretto is based. But these are tenuous connections. It is better to say that Auden's ultimate distinction between eros and agape is that eros can find some indirect means of expression, while agape must be experienced and not spoken about. "I never suspected the way of truth / Was a way of silence" (CP 409). But how does one *say* that one must be silent?[16] Auden seeks to answer that question is his extraordinarily reticent, and extraordinarily powerful, poem about agape, "Friday's Child." The word "love" appears only once in the poem; genuine agape is attributed to Dietrich Bonhoeffer only in the title, and there only by implication—Auden assumes that we know that "Friday's child is loving and giving," assumes also that we understand how the old Mother Goose rhyme draws on the memory of Good Friday, when God loved and gave most fully. The poem concludes with an invocation, and a recommendation, of silence in the face of an evil that cannot be comprehended and a faith that, as Kierkegaard said, can be neither explained nor justified:

Now, did He really break the seal
And rise again? We dare not say;
But conscious unbelievers feel
    Quite sure of Judgement Day.

Meanwhile, a silence on the cross,
As dead as we shall ever be,
Speaks of some total gain or loss,
    And you and I are free

To guess from the insulted face
Just what Appearances He saves
By suffering in a public place
    A death reserved for slaves.   (CP 676)

The key phrase here is "We dare not say." It is not the same as "We dare not believe," though whether Auden actually believed in the bodily resurrection at this point in his life is hard to tell.[17] It is probably not the same as "We dare not proclaim," since undoubtedly Auden often did proclaim, in church at least, "On the third day he rose again in accordance with the Scriptures." More likely, he means that we dare not affirm this as a statement of what is the case, we dare not present it for rational scrutiny and evaluation according to accepted canons of evidence and probability. As Auden said repeatedly, almost obsessively, "Orthodoxy is reticence"; orthodoxy, especially in matters of love, is knowing when to shut up.[18]

CHAPTER 6

Ariel and the Menippea

O how the devil who controls
The moral asymmetric souls,
The either-ors, the mongrel halves
Who find truth in a mirror, laughs.
Yet time and memory are still
Limiting factors on his will;
He cannot always fool us thrice,
For he may never tell us lies,
Just half-truths we can synthesise.
So, hidden in his hocus-pocus,
There lies the gift of double focus,
That magic lamp which looks so dull
And utterly impractical
Yet, if Aladdin use it right,
Can be a sesame to light.

—"NEW YEAR LETTER"

Throughout his career Auden considered it bad news to hear that someone was writing about his poetry, but in 1963, Monroe Spears surprised him by producing a critical study of which he approved. "No author could hope for a more conscientious and generous consideration of his work," he wrote to Spears after seeing the proofs and added the comment quoted in this book's introduction: "I am particularly pleased that you seem to perceive, what I hoped was there, a continuity and development of an outlook on the world, not a succession of unrelated ideologies" (Berg Collection). Auden's conviction of his "continuity" of purpose and concern has rarely been endorsed by his critics; and in some ways the present study could be thought to contribute to the sense of divergence and rupture in Auden's career. Yet Auden's claims to continuity of development are valid. One underlying argument of this book has been that the upheavals in his life, and in the world around him, enabled Auden to see more clearly the direction his thought and his work had already been headed for some years; such insight in turn enabled him to pursue that direction with more conscious determination and with, as the years went by, a remarkable imperviousness to the protests of his increasingly disappointed or outraged critics. There is much to be said for Stephen Spender's verdict on the Auden of the late 1940s, in his memoir *World Within World*: "If Auden's changes of view seemed sometimes like the abrupt changes of a kaleidoscope into a new pattern unconnected with any previous one (except that the instrument and the pieces which form the patterns were the same), his own life showed more unity of purpose throughout the twenty years since we were at Oxford than that of any of my friends. . . . Auden had developed and yet remained the same person" (272–73).

Still, to turn the argument around once more, certain kinds of continuity can be misleading—as can be certain kinds of change. It would be possible for a poet to adopt a new style, or to begin to work in new genres, because she saw opportunities to pursue more strongly a vision of poetry which she had long held and intended to maintain. It would be equally possible for the same poet to develop a wholly new purpose or vision for her poetry, which would nevertheless allow her to continue using the same forms and working within the same style.

Both of these examples fit Auden. For instance, in chapter 4 I argued that his sympathy for local forms of culture had been developing for several years before, in "New Year Letter," he began to articulate it clearly and directly. Similarly, Auden exhibited certain generic tendencies and preferences throughout his career, but not always for the same reasons. Of special interest here is Auden's status, early and late, as one of the great modern masters of the genre variously called the anatomy or the menippean satire. His understanding of the importance of this genre, or rather of the ideological preferences which it embodies, is best approached through a further exploration of Auden's psychomachian interpretation of *The Tempest*.

Ariel doesn't have much to say in *The Sea and the Mirror*. He is spoken *to* at some length by Prospero and spoken *for* by the loquacious Caliban, but in the end only has thirty lines of his own to intone (fewer than even the stage manager), and Prospero himself produces, studded in his long-lined meditative verse, three Arielesque lyrics, each roughly as long as Ariel's one little number. One might imagine that Auden had read a version of *The Tempest* with the songs left out. Without the magnificent "Full fathom five" and "Where the bee sucks, there suck I" to sing, not much would be left to poor Ariel. And so it is in *The Sea and the Mirror*. On first glance it appears that Auden does at least give Ariel the last word, brief though that word be, but in fact his airy song is echoed by another: it is the prompter who closes the poem with his potentially sardonic summary of Ariel's message: " . . . I" In short, Auden does everything but close Ariel out of his "commentary" altogether. Why?

Later in Auden's career he would make a habit of classifying poets as "Ariel-dominated" or "Prospero-dominated." This distinction must be kept clearly in mind by anyone who wants to understand *The Sea and the Mirror;* it is one to which we will return. Auden explains his little scheme most fully and explicitly in his essay on Robert Frost, first published in *The Dyer's Hand* but apparently given (in an earlier incarnation) as a lecture during Auden's tenure as Oxford's Professor of Poetry in 1957:

> The Grecian Urn states Ariel's position ["Beauty is truth, truth beauty"]; Prospero's has been equally succinctly stated by Dr. Johnson: *The only end of writing is to enable the readers better to enjoy life or better to endure it.*
>
> We want a poem to be beautiful, that is to say, a verbal earthly paradise, a timeless world of pure play, which gives us delight precisely because of its contrast to our historical existence with all its insoluble

problems and all its inescapable suffering; at the same time we want a poem to be true, that is to say, to provide us with some kind of revelation about our life which will show us what life is really like and free us from self-enchantment and deception, and a poet cannot bring us any truth without introducing into his poetry the problematic, the painful, the disorderly, the ugly.   (DH 338)[1]

With the Prospero-dominated poetry described at the end of that quotation we have been much occupied in this study; Auden spent a good deal of his career searching for a way, as a poet, to do what Prospero wants to do—to teach, to warn, to exhort—without succumbing to the arrogance of believing that he can thereby become one of the "unacknowledged legislators of the world." But Auden's relationship to Ariel-dominated poetry is equally central to his self-understanding and equally complicated.

"Beauty is truth, truth beauty." Auden didn't think so, and on these grounds dissociated himself most explicitly from Ariel-poetry. For a third time let us note Auden's very important story about how he chose a "buddle" for his "Platonic Idea of a concentrating mill": "One type I found more sacred or 'beautiful,' but the other type was, as I knew from my reading, the more efficient. At this point I realized that it was my moral duty to sacrifice my aesthetic preference to reality or truth" (*Certain* 425). If one could convincingly posit the union of beauty and truth, then this sort of problem would never arise. But Auden knew that life is never as simple as the urn would have us believe, and that the poet, like the aesthetically sensitive mining engineer, is regularly faced with dilemmas of just this kind.

None of the poets whom Auden thought of as his masters or as models wrote the kind of poetry which he identifies with Ariel—poems like George Peele's "Bathsabe's Song" (from a play called *The Love of King David and Fair Bathsabe*, though in his essay on the characteristically Prosperan poet Robert Frost, Auden presents it simply as a lyric):

Hot sun, cool fire, tempered with sweet air,
Black shade, fair nurse, shadow my white hair:

Shine, sun; burn, fire; breathe, air, and ease me;
Black shade, fair nurse, shroud me and please me:
Shadow, my sweet nurse, keep me from burning,
Make not my glad cause, cause for mourning.
    Let not my beauty's fire
    Inflame unstaid desire,
    Nor pierce any bright eye
    That wandereth lightly.

The "I" of this poem, Auden writes, "seems anonymous, hardly more than a grammatical form; one cannot imagine meeting Bathsabe at a dinner party" (DH 339). In short, it is the kind of incantatory poem that has led some critics over the years to think of the lyric as, in the words of Daniel Albright, "the most anonymous and universalized of literary forms"; and Albright is surely right to point out that Auden could have chosen as an equally fine example of such pure and meaning-free poetry Ariel's own "Full fathom five," since as a means of informing a man about the death of his father it leaves something to be desired (*Lyricality* 28).

Again, this is not the sort of poem written by Auden's masters: neither Pope nor Hardy—nor Horace, for that matter— is often celebrated for pure verbal musicianship. And, as we noted in the previous chapter, after Auden discovered opera he became more and more convinced that *here* was the place for verbal music, not on the printed page, or even in the lecture hall: "no speaking voice, however magnificent, can hope to compete, in expressiveness through sound, with a great singing voice backed by an orchestra" (DH 26). Even Auden's famous metrical virtuosity was not normally put in the service of obviously musical effects: in a 1962 letter to Elizabeth Mayer about his poem "Thanksgiving for a Habitat" he wrote, "To keep the diction and rhythm within a hairsbreadth of being prose without becoming it is a task I find very difficult" (Carpenter 419). But there is another side to this story. The previous chapter treated the means by which Auden worked the expressions of erotic love into his verse, and given the important relations between the erotic and the lyrical, that discussion could be as it were transcribed into another key: what was said there about the erotic could be said here about the lyrical. Auden was perfectly capable of writing exquisitely Arielesque lines when he so chose; but he would typically give them a narrative context (as in "As I walked out one evening"), or hedge them about with ironic quotation marks (as in "O the valley in the summer where I and my John"), or place them within the dramatic context of the opera.

In each case the lyrical is juxtaposed with or subsumed under another genre, an operation that can best be executed in literary or aesthetic forms that lend themselves to the mixing of genres. And the opera is perhaps the ultimate mixed form: it not only combines prose and verse in its words, but further combines those words with music and spectacle (*lexis* with *melos* and *opsis*, as Aristotle says in the *Poetics* —and the tragedies he knew were, in performance, considerably closer to Verdi than to Ibsen). The constantly shifting importance of these elements, not only from opera to opera, but from moment to moment *within* a given opera, resonates profoundly with a tendency which I believe characterizes Auden from the beginning of his career to the end: a resistance to any genre, and any system of thought, that too precisely defines, too rigidly excludes, too methodically organizes.

But there are many possible motives for such resistance. One cannot help suspecting that one of the most important services Auden's preference for mixed forms performed for him, especially in the thirties, was to provide a certain protective coloration. For instance, at the conclusion of Auden's "masque," *The Dance of Death*, immediately after the death of the dancer, "Mr Karl Marx" appears on stage, welcomed by the chorus singing these words to the tune of Mendelssohn's "Wedding March":

> O Mr Marx, you've gathered
> All the material facts
> You know the economic
> Reasons for our acts.

Then Marx concludes the play with this pronouncement: "The instruments of production have been too much for him. He is liquidated" (*Plays and Other Dramatic Writings* 107).

Edward Mendelson has written that "any Marxist who found this satisfying was deaf to irony" (*Early* 270); but this comment is less obviously true in the context of the play than it is to the reader of the ending alone. This conclusion is perfectly in keeping with the overall tone of the work, which makes heavy use of the more farcical elements of both the German cabaret and British musical-hall entertainment. Some audiences—perhaps the audiences that attended the Group Theatre productions in the thirties—might find it perfectly appropriate that a play which symbolically represents the death of the bourgeoisie as a class would repudiate that class's notions of dramatic "seriousness" and replace them with an aesthetic drawn from artistic genres preferred by the working class.[2] And perhaps Auden felt the same way when he wrote the play, even though in 1942 he scribbled in a friend's copy of the play the comment that "the communists never spotted that this was a nihilistic leg-pull" (Mendelson, *Early* 270).[3] One wonders if here, as so often elsewhere, Auden allowed his memory to resolve what was at the time a real ambivalence. Certainly he was at the time of writing *The Dance of Death* (1933) profoundly ambivalent about the possible social and political functions of art.

What seems, on the face of it, more odd is that after he became a Christian—and, as we have seen, one element of his conversion was his repudiation of all leftist dreams for the central role of art in shaping the coming New Jerusalem—he maintained his preference for mixed forms. It is true that in the forties the note of music-hall buffoonery largely disappears from his longer work (the earliest of the libretti, *Paul Bunyan*, retaining more of it than anything that would follow), but he continues to alternate serious and frivolous passages, juxtapose verse and prose, and employ an astonishing variety of verse forms.

Eliot provides an illuminating counter-example to this tendency. Now, it would be hard to believe that Auden's understanding of the possibilities of mixed forms and genres was not shaped to a great degree by his reading of *The Waste Land*. Moreover, it was Eliot himself who had argued, in his essay "The Possibility of a Poetic Drama," for a new poetic drama modeled in part on the English music hall (*Sacred* 70)—whose great artist, Eliot claimed in another famous essay, was Marie Lloyd (*Selected* 405–8). But by the time he began devoting his attention chiefly to the drama—as can be seen in his 1951 lecture "Poetry and Drama"—Eliot had come to believe that if possible there should be no mixing of verse and prose in drama. Such transitions, while they may have been appropriate for an Elizabethan audience, are for the modern audience too jarring and distracting: "we have to accustom our audiences to verse to the point at which they will cease to be conscious of it" (*On Poetry* 78). Clearly, Eliot is seeking a more seamless form of art, one that depends on continuity and flow rather than the discontinuities and impediments that characterized *The Waste Land* (about which he was so dismissive in his later years). One could argue that such a decision is ideologically appropriate for a poet who has embraced Christian orthodoxy and who thereby has come to see in the world itself a singular teleological thrust, propelled by the sovereignty of God.

Why, then, does the Christian Auden continue to employ mixed forms with an undiminished vigor? It is necessary to look more closely at the character of these mixed genres and then at Auden's use of them.

One genre, or generic complex, is key for an understanding of Auden: the menippean satire or menippea, also called (by Northrop Frye and his followers) the anatomy. Frye and Mikhail Bakhtin are the two great celebrants, among modern critics, of this literary tradition, and they have defined it better than anyone else. According to Frye,

> The Menippean satire deals less with people as such than with mental attitudes. Pedants, bigots, cranks, parvenus, virtuosi, enthusiasts, rapacious and incompetent professional men of all kinds, are handled in terms of their occupational approach to life as distinct from their social behavior. The Menippean satire thus resembles the confession in its ability to handle abstract ideas and theories, and differs from the novel in its characterization, which is stylized rather than naturalistic, and presents people as mouthpieces of the ideas they represent. . . . The novelist sees evil and folly as social diseases, but the Menippean satirist sees them as diseases of the intellect. (*Anatomy* 309)

This description fits Auden's approach to characterization with a remarkable precision. Examples could be taken from virtually any point in his career. In 1929 he and Isherwood drafted a "Preliminary Statement" describing their dramatic theory, in which Auden wrote "Dramatic 'characters' are always abstractions" (*Plays and Other Dramatic Writings* 459). It's telling that Isherwood, the novelist-to-be, deleted this statement in the manuscript; certainly, in his collaborations with Auden, Isherwood pulled him away from abstraction and toward more naturalistic portrayals. But as soon as Auden is working alone—as in *The Dance of Death*—the love of abstractions and personifications returns with a vengeance. More than a decade later, Jung's four elemental psychological faculties (Intuition, Feeling, Sensation, and Thought) appear in the "Annunciation" section of *For the Time Being* (CP 355–61), and then reappear as the four characters of *The Age of Anxiety* (Quant, Rosetta, Emble, and Malin). And Auden and Kallman produced in 1965 some program notes for their libretto to *The Bassarids* which directly explain the religious position that each of the main characters represents: Tiersias pursues "the latest thing in religious fashion," Agave "believes in nothing," the god that Pentheus "has come to believe in is one, universal, and impersonal, the Good," and so on (L 699–700).

It could scarcely be more clear, then, that Auden worked throughout his career in the menippean tradition of characterization—which may be one reason why some critics have found his longer works so difficult and unpleasing. Larkin, for instance, wrote of *The Age of Anxiety* that "I never finished it"—note the finality of the past tense there: had he said "I *have* never finished it" another go would seem possible—"and have never met anyone who has" (126), while the same poem made Jarrell almost apoplectic (but, as always, hilariously so): "it is the equivalent of Wordsworth's 'Ecclesiastical Sonnets.' The man who, during the thirties, was one of the five or six best poets in the world has gradually turned into a rhetoric mill grinding away at the bottom of Limbo, into an automaton that keeps making little jokes, little plays on words, little rhetorical engines, as compulsively and unendingly and uneasily as a neurotic washes his hands" (*Kipling* 145). Jarrell's emphasis on the words "rhetoric" and "rhetorical" betrays his uneasiness (not Auden's) with poems that are neither lyrical nor in any conventional sense narrational: though *The Age of Anxiety* is in one sense a quest narrative, it does not follow the conventions of quest romance in either its plot or its characterizations; and it is certainly no epic. Because Larkin and Jarrell were unfamiliar with the tradition in which Auden was working—or at least did not recognize it in this case—they could only conclude that he was trying to write other kinds of poetry and making an enormous hash of it. No wonder, then, that they were so puzzled at what appeared to be a dramatic fall into incompetence. In fact, Auden had chosen the appropriate generic form for what he wished to accomplish in *The Age of Anxiety*, a taxonomic inquiry into the disintegration of human minds in late modernity. Thus Bakhtin:

> In the menippea there appears for the first time what might be called moral-psychological experimentation: a representation of the unusual, abnormal moral and psychic states of man—insanity of all sorts (the theme of the maniac), split personality, unrestrained daydreaming, unusual dreams, passions bordering on madness, suicides, and so forth. These phenomena do not function narrowly in the menippea as mere themes, but have a formal generic significance. Dreams, daydreams, insanity destroy the epic and tragic wholeness of a person and his fate: the possibilities of another person and another life are revealed in him, he loses his finalized quality and ceases to mean only one thing; he ceases to coincide with himself.   (*Problems* 116–17)

This is a wonderfully precise description of how Auden handles characterization in *The Age of Anxiety*, where the borders between the conscious and the unconscious are constantly being erased; where waking cannot be distinguished from dreaming (and let us remember that the alliterative verse which dominates the poem is derived from perhaps the greatest dream vision in English literature, *Piers Plowman*), in which persons not only interact but seem to bleed into one another. *The Age of Anxiety* is not, I think, one of Auden's better poems; but most of the condemnation it has received has been perpe-trated by people who had not the faintest idea what tradition Auden was working in.

In more general terms, it is scarcely surprising that Auden would find the menippea appealing. Some of his favorite writers worked in this tradition: Frye, in fact singles out two of them, Lewis Carroll and Kierkegaard (specifically, *Either/Or*) as modern examples of the menippean tradition (310, 313). One might add W. S. Gilbert, whose influence on Auden's early poetic dramas is enormous. But the menippea's interest for Auden was multiplex, as can be seen through an unpacking of some of Bakhtin's comments on the early centuries of the genre:

> Characteristic of the menippea is a wide use of inserted genres . . .
> [and] its concern with current and topical issues. This is, in its own way,
> the "journalistic" genre of antiquity, acutely echoing the ideological
> issues of the day.   (*Problems* 118)

The menippea, moreover, "is a genre of 'ultimate questions.' In it ulti-mate philosophical presuppositions are put to the test" (115). But this testing is reluctant to culminate in a direct answer, a resolution of the questions it raises: it "serves not for the positive *embodiment* of truth, but as a mode of searching after truth, provoking it" (114). Thus those readers or hearers of *The Dance of Death* who believed "Mr Karl Marx" to be giving the final and unquestionable word on the events that had just occurred were (like Larkin and Jarrell later) ignorant of the genre in which Auden was working—and of, as well, Auden's own conflicted political position, and the pure pleasure he took in meeting the technical demands of various "inserted genres." (It must also be said that Auden did nothing to clear up these misapprehensions, since as long as his ambivalence was unperceived he could receive no criti-cism for it.)

The menippea is also, Bakhtin emphasizes, a (or perhaps the) fundamentally carnivalesque genre: "Menippean satire became one of the main carriers and channels for the carnival sense of the world in literature, and remains so to the present day" (113). This is especially interesting in light of Auden's later fascination with carnival, which seems to have arisen from his work (along with Elizabeth Mayer) as translator of Goethe's *Italian Journey*.[4] Goethe was in Rome during the carnival season in 1788, and wrote at some length about what he saw there. He confines himself chiefly to a documentary record of the festivities, though he does conclude, on Ash Wednesday, with some reflections, in a *tempis fugit* spirit, on the end of the carnival:

> In so concluding my Ash Wednesday meditation, I trust that I have not saddened my readers. Such was very far from my intention. On the contrary, knowing that life, taken as a whole, is like the Roman Carnival, unpredictable, unsatisfactory and problematic, I hope that this carefree crowd of maskers will make them remember how valuable is every moment of joy, however fleeting and trivial it may seem to be. (470)

Perhaps this reflection caught Auden's attention, for in a late review which describes the meaning of carnival he strikes the same note, though in a Kierkegaardian and Christian rather than Goethe's pagan spirit:

> Carnival celebrates the unity of our human race as mortal creatures, who come into this world and depart from it without our consent, who must eat, drink, defecate, belch, and break wind in order to live, and procreate if our species is to survive. Our feelings about this are ambiguous. To us as individuals, it is a cause for rejoicing to know that we are not alone, that all of us, irrespective of age or sex or rank or talent, are in the same boat. As unique persons, on the other hand, all of us are resentful that an exception cannot be made in our own case. We oscillate between wishing we were unreflective animals and wishing we were disembodied spirits, for in either case we should not be problematic to ourselves. The Carnival solution of this ambiguity is to laugh, for laughter is simultaneously a protest and an acceptance. (F&A 471)

This is the Horatian Auden talking, the man who wishes to " 'look at / this world with a happy eye / but from a sober perspective' " (CP 773): he accepts the world and gives thanks for it, but to do that properly he must also accept and give thanks for his own instinct to protest against injustice and complain about constrictions. This is a complex imperative, so complex that it cannot be contained by what Bakhtin called the "totalizing" and "monological" tendencies of the "high and straightforward" genres such as epic and tragedy.

Not surprisingly, Auden may sometimes be found engaging in direct or indirect critique of the monology of the epic: "The Shield of Achilles" (CP 596–98) portrays those elements of the historical world which even Homer, with his comprehensive aerial vision (so like that of the aviator whom Auden in his early poems loved to impersonate) failed to see and note, indeed was not able to see: "The eyes of the crow and the eye of the camera," he writes in another poem of the same period, "open / Onto Homer's world, not ours" (591). Which is another way of saying that Homer sees only what the camera and the crow see, not this vision, accessible only to the eye of moral understanding:

> A ragged urchin, aimless and alone,
>> Loitered about that vacancy; a bird
> Flew up to safety from his well-aimed stone:
>> That girls are raped, that two boys knife a third,
>> Were axioms to him, who'd never heard
> Of any world where promises were kept,
> Or one could weep because another wept.   (CP 598)

Likewise, though more lightly, "Secondary Epic" chastises Virgil for his narrow singularity of vision, in which even Asian rivers are "Learning to flow in a latinate style" (599) and we are asked to believe that "the first of the Romans can learn / His Roman history in the future tense" (598). To such claims Auden must say, twice, "No, Virgil, no," and offer as a counterbalancing voice a Petronian, a menippean, scribe, a "down-at-heels refugee rhetorician / With an empty belly, seeking employment" (599) who, four centuries or so after Virgil, sells a very different interpretation to a Teutonic

>> princeling whom loot had inclined
> To believe that providence had assigned
> To blonds the task of improving mankind.   (599)

In this fellow's poetic history—no more revisionist than that by which Virgil made Homer's Greeks the villains, his Trojans the destined (if belated) victors—the Roman Empire becomes the inevitably defeated antagonist, *"As two-horned Rhine throws off the Latin yoke"* and *"Alaric has avenged Turnus."* It turns out that the shield of Aeneas failed to tell the whole story after all. What could be more Bakhtinian, or more characteristic of the subversive, un-totalizing, anti-totalitarian genres that Bakhtin loved?

The epic cannot contain history, for precisely the same reasons the physical world of the given moment cannot be contained by the genre of scientific discourse. Which is why, in "Ode to Terminus," Auden links Prosperian poetic hubris—including his own—with the arrogance of the modern scientist and wishes that both could come under the sway of Terminus, "God of walls, doors and reticence":

> In this world our colossal immodesty
> has plundered and poisoned, it is possible
>   You still might save us, who by now have
>   learned this: that scientists, to be truthful,
>
> must remind us to take all they say as a
> tall story, that abhorred in the Heav'ns are all
>   self-proclaimed poets who, to wow an
>   audience, utter some resonant lie.   (CP 811)

(It is likely that Auden has a "resonant lie" of his own in mind here, "September 1, 1939"; see the appendix.) Bakhtin again provides the best gloss on this theme. Writing of the "serio-comic" genres, most notable among them the menippean satire, he argues that "parodic-travestying literature introduces the permanent corrective of laughter, of a critique on the one-sided seriousness of the lofty direct word, the corrective of reality that is always richer, more fundamental and most importantly *too contradictory and heteroglot* to be fit into a high and straightforward genre" (*Dialogic* 55).

In this spirit, one of the notable tendencies of Auden's later light verse is to suggest not the inaccuracy but the insufficiency of scientific descriptions of human life. Also in "Ode to Terminus," for example, he points out that a world in which the sun's "light is felt as a friendly / presence not a photonic bombardment" is "the world we / really live in," and this "saves our sanity" (CP 810). In "After Reading a Child's Guide to Modern Physics" he ruminates on the same divergence of perspectives:

> Though the face at which I stare
> While shaving it be cruel
> For, year after year, it repels
> An ageing suitor, it has,
> Thank God, sufficient mass
> To be altogether there,
> Not an indeterminate gruel
> Which is partly somewhere else.   (CP 740–41)

One can see similar reflections in, among other poems, Auden's "New Year Greeting" to the bacteria inhabiting his body (CP 837) and in his commentary on the first "Moon Landing" (CP 843). Yet is it absolutely essential to understand that this recurrent theme does not in any way indicate a disrespect for or disbelief in science. No modern poet was more scientifically literate than Auden, or more convinced of the importance of scientific literacy.[5] But it was precisely this knowledge of science that enabled him to understand that scientific discourse tends to make claims—for the range, the extensiveness, and the exclusivity of its knowledge—that scientific activity cannot fully support. The "corrective of laughter" was therefore needed, not in order to discredit science, but in order to situate it among the discourses which collectively describe our world.

In this context it is worth remembering that the carnivalesque spirit, the spirit of the menippean satire and of Auden's light verse, is neither nihilistic nor cynical, nor even necessarily skeptical. (For this reason the Bakhtinian description of carnival has been misappropriated by adherents of deconstruction.) Bakhtin again:

> Ancient parody was free of any nihilistic denial. It was not, after all, the heroes who were parodied, nor the Trojan War and its participants;

what was parodied was only its epic heroization; not Hercules and his exploits but their tragic heroization. The genre itself, the style, the language are all put in cheerfully irreverent quotation marks, and they are perceived against a backdrop of contradictory reality that cannot be confined within their narrow frames. The direct and serious word was revealed, in all its limitations and insufficiency, only after it had become the laughing image of that word—but it was by no means discredited in the process.   (*Dialogic* 55–56)

Precisely the same is true of the Christian carnivalesque, the "great parodic-travestying literature of the Middle Ages" and its liturgical and celebratory analogues. It is only in the modern world that "the functions of parody [have become] narrow and unproductive. Parody has grown sickly, its place in modern literature is insignificant" (71). Auden, though, is working in the older tradition. On just this subject he writes,

In medieval carnivals, parodies of the rituals of the Church were common, but what Lewis Carroll said of literary parody—"One can only parody a poem one admires"—is true of all parody. One can only blaspheme if one believes. The world of Laughter is much more closely related to the world of Worship and Prayer than either is to the everyday, secular world of Work.   (F&A 472)

One can see the relation of these themes to some of the points made in earlier chapters of this book: the homoerotic love that threatens the spirit less than the idolatry to which Tristan and Isolde succumb; the members of a provincial operatic troupe who find their blessedness through recognizing their ineptitude; the city that becomes its own vision through failing to achieve its self-expectations. In each case what Auden calls us to do is to laugh—not to flee from love or art or the City, not to succumb to despair, not to pretend to a greater glory than we have indeed achieved; but simply to laugh. Laughter does not undo commitment, any more than parody undoes or refutes the greatness of a poem (Auden did not find Homer and Virgil inferior poets), but rather eases the burdens that accompany, and may enfeeble or even fracture, commitment.

Eliot wrote, more than once, that Christianity makes strict demands but has low expectations (see Ricks 204); laughter, for Auden, is found in the recognition of the gap between demand and expectation. One could put this in another, more traditionally theological, way by saying that the law's high demands are not abrogated but fulfilled in the gospel of love (the agape of our previous chapter), which expects nothing from people but an admission of failure and a plea for forgiveness. This is the point that Auden makes when he finds Christ figures not in the usual places, but in Shakespeare's Falstaff and in Wodehouse's Jeeves: "So speaks comically—and in what mode other than the comic could it on earth truthfully speak?—the voice of Agape, of Holy Love" (DH 145). For the later Auden the use of mixed genres is imperative largely because it promotes the kinds of contradictions that make us laugh; and they make us laugh because they indicate a reality "too contradictory and heteroglot" to be subsumed under any single literary genre, however expansive and culturally authoritative.

The early Auden's equally strong preference for the mixed genres, it seems to me, is prompted by a preliminary intuition of the same idea, a sense that none of the reigning ideologies (psychoanalysis, Marxism, Christianity as he then understood it) was able to live up to its universal claims or justify its totalizing impulses. The early Auden's mania for charts, noted in chapter 1, is an attempt to make a whole by bricolage, piecing together the various fragments that had masqueraded as wholes. Such an activity is also a token of simple confusion, and an attempt to discover whether the competing ideologies are as fragmentary and incommensurable as they give every appearance of being—"Just half-truths we can synthesize," as the "New Year Letter" has it (CP 220). Earlier I noted, parenthetically, that the politically minded Auden of the mid-thirties could not be chastised for his ambivalence as long as it remained unrecognized, and this is a point that Michael Sidnell develops nicely: writing about the "Shakespearian pastiche" in Auden's contributions to *The Ascent of F6*, he argues that "in such verse Auden seemed to be working both sides of the stylistic street. If it was taken at face value as the language of poetic tragedy (as it often was) well and good; if not, the bolt hole of burlesque had been prepared" (204). It may be that Auden was prepared to leave such decisions to his readers because he himself could not say whether the verse he had written was tragic or burlesque; just as he may well have been unable to say, in 1933, whether Marx's entrance at the end of *The Dance of Death* is the true verdict on the demise of the bourgeoisie or a "nihilistic leg-pull." Christianity would later provide an ideological justification for mixed forms—one might say even a commandment to use them, as a way of enforcing epistemological as well as moral humility—but the pre-Christian Auden has very different reasons for exercising the very same preferences. Sidnell is thus right in at least two senses when he says that "Drama was Auden's element" (62). However furiously Auden may have worked in notebooks and in prose writings to put the cultural Humpty-Dumpty together again, in drama he could organize and display the pieces as a loose mosaic of, yes, pieces. Any reader or viewer who saw one piece as the central one, or the right one, or the key to understanding the others, was free to do so. It was only after Auden became a Christian that he could perceive the confusion as resulting not only from the world's disorder but also from our own, and to understand it as a salutary reminder of our finitude rather than a temporary impediment to our construction of Utopia. "For now we see through a glass darkly, but then"—and only then—"face to face."

Afterword

We never step twice into the same Auden.

—HERACLITUS (AS QUOTED BY
RANDALL JARRELL, "FREUD TO PAUL")

*One normally reacts to Auden as to the insistent person-
ality of an actor-manager recognisable as his own familiar
self whatever part he plays.*

—FRANÇOIS DUCHÊNE, *THE CASE
OF THE HELMETED AIRMAN*

Seamus Heaney has written of Auden, "his career represents the full
turn of the wheel from his initial rejection of a milieu and a tradition
to his final complaisant incorporation within them" (110–11). Let us
leave aside the tendentious word "complaisant"—though Heaney is
not using it in the usual pejorative sense—and focus on "milieu" and
"tradition." Does Heaney mean that Auden began his career by rejecting a *particular* milieu or tradition? If so, he is right: while Auden does
not employ the "strenuous adversary gestures" (Fussell 212) of the
high modernists he nevertheless chooses a different path than theirs.
Indeed, one could say that Auden takes an adversarial position towards
modernism simply by refusing to take an adversarial position towards
anything else. But by virtue of this very point, Heaney is wrong if he
means that Auden began his career by repudiating poetic milieus and

traditions *tout court*. It would be more accurate to say—as several chapters in this book, especially the third, have shown—that Auden was more interested in renovating old and neglected traditions than in inventing new ones. For instance, chapter 6 noted that Auden's first dramatic work, *Paid on Both Sides*, draws on the mummer's play; it also uses an alliterative verse form based on Anglo-Saxon poetry and, as Edward Mendelson has noted, takes its title from a line in *Beowulf* (P xiv). Likewise, in a 1929 journal (EA 301) Auden invokes as a model for his dramatic work Hrotswitha, a tenth-century Benedictine abbess who herself practiced the resuscitation of old literary forms: according to *The Oxford Companion to English Literature*, she "adapted the comedies of Terence [!] for the use of her convent."

Auden always understood himself, as a poet and a thinker, to be in the position of heir. Eliot famously said that tradition "cannot be inherited, and if you want it you must obtain it by great labour" (*Selected* 4), but I think Auden would say that you will inherit some tradition whether you want to or not. Tradition, as Gadamer says, is "not what we do or ought to do, but what happens to us over and above our wanting and doing" (xxviii). Auden could at times suffer from the anxiety of influence, especially in his relations with Yeats (see Callan's chapter 10), but in general he seems to have thought in much less combative terms about his relations to his poetic predecessors. Describing his early poetic career he would refer to Thomas Hardy as his "Master" (DH 38), in precisely the sense in which one might refer to a master carpenter or a master stonemason or—to choose the analogy Auden would probably have preferred, given his half-fanciful description of what poetic apprenticeship should be like—a master sculptor or painter in Renaissance Florence:

> If poetry were in great public demand so that there were overworked professional poets, I can imagine a system under which an established poet would take on a small number of apprentices who would begin by changing his blotting paper, advance to typing his manuscripts and end up by ghostwriting poems for him which he was too busy to start or finish. The apprentices might really learn something for, knowing that he would get the blame as well as the credit for their work, the

Master would be extremely choosy about his apprentices and do his best to teach them all he knew.   (DH 37)

If for Harold Bloom and many post-Romantic poets the dominant metaphor in their thinking about poetic history is that of the *family* (especially the Freudian family romance), for Auden it is that of the *guild*. This is one reason why Alasdair MacIntyre's thinking about traditions is so useful in the consideration of Auden's career; MacIntyre understands that every social practice, including poetry, is tradition-generated and tradition-bound.

In the introduction I noted a distinction between the Eliotic use of the big word "Tradition" with Auden's (and MacIntyre's) use of the much smaller word "traditions." In the Eliotic vocabulary Tradition is something heroically chosen and then, much later and after titanic struggle, fully and genuinely achieved; but traditions, while they may also be chosen, assert a constant shaping pressure on the person which constrains and directs his or her choices. (Gadamer's usage, in the sentence quoted above, is closer to MacIntyre's than to Eliot's, though Gadamer employs the singular.) Our traditions envelop and to a degree constitute us, so much so that we are never wholly free to choose. Auden believed wholeheartedly that his having been "born and bred / a British Pharisee" (CP 774) made certain choices impossible for him, which is one reason why he could never accept that Christopher Isherwood was perfectly serious in his embrace of Eastern religion (Carpenter 320–21). And yet within those socially constructed limits choice was not only possible but morally mandatory.

However mistaken he may have been about Isherwood, Auden consistently avoided, almost from the beginning of his career and certainly to its end, the twin temptations of Pelagius and Calvin: radical voluntarism and radical determinism. Though he loved Kierkegaard, he was well aware that the emphasis Kierkegaard placed on the solitary deliberative mind prevented him from seeing that social institutions shape that mind's choices—indeed, make choice itself possible: "The Danish Lutheran Church may have been as worldly as Kierkegaard thought it was, but if it had not existed he would never have heard of the Gospels, in which he found the standards by which he condemned it" (F&A 189). But Auden was equally well aware that his theological inclination to "a Barthian exaggeration of God's transcendence all too easily becomes an excuse for complacency about one's own sins and about the misfortunes of others" (*Religion* 25). One must be careful, then, not to overstress the deterministic or fatalistic note in Auden's work, as I believe Stan Smith and Seamus Heaney, in their different ways, both do. When Heaney insists that Auden sought a break with tradition, "an escape from the given," he goes on to claim that Auden "insists upon the necessity of these acts of self-liberation only to expose their ultimately illusory promise" (110); and just as I think that Heaney exaggerates Auden's discomfort with tradition, I also think that he exaggerates Auden's fatalism about choice. It is necessary to recognize, as several commentators have noted and has been seen from time to time in this study, Auden's fondness for paradoxical statements about the relation between choice and necessity:

> We live in freedom by necessity.... (CP 194)

> O hold us to the voluntary way.... (SP 115)

> Where Freedom dwells because it must,
> Necessity because it can.... (CP 240)

Those of us who were trained in New Critical principles, or some attenuated version thereof, were tensioned and paradoxed to within an inch of our lives and thus find it hard even to hear such language anymore. But since the critical pendulum has, in the last twenty years, swung so far from the voluntarism that reigned in the heyday of the existentialists (among whom should be counted some, especially American, proponents of deconstruction), surely there is something to be said for Auden's attempt at negotiating among the several and competing forces—including the personal will—that may plausibly be said to act upon human lives.

That last paragraph may be considered an extension of the argument of chapter 6, since it constitutes another way of formulating an explanation for Auden's love of the mixed genres. And if anything is true of Auden from the beginning of his career to the end, it is that commitment to artistic and critical acknowledgment of the need for constant negotiation among powerful self-shaping forces.

That, and one more thing. I have sometimes said to myself as I wrote this book that I will never again write about anyone so damnably smart. In delineating and critiquing two major strands of Romanticism; in conducting, over a period of decades, a genealogical inquiry into and rehabilitation of the Horatians; in repudiating Marxism's totalizations in favor of a Hellenic-cum-Christian understanding of the City and citizenship; in interrogating Freudian and post-Freudian theories of the erotic and finding them, as compared to the Christian tradition's articulation of agape and its consequent situating of the erotic, wanting; in exercising a lifelong suspicion of the monological genres, and in pursuing their dialogical counterparts—in all these strict and focused investigations Auden exhibits an intelligence so remarkable that one can understand, even if one recoils from such boldness, why Joseph Brodsky called Auden "the greatest mind of the twentieth century" (357).

What remains, and will remain, matter for debate is the validity of the conclusions that this great mind came to during its many years of honorable wrestling. I have quarreled a bit with Seamus Heaney in these last few pages, but no one, it seems to me, has stated nearly so well, so fairly and so justly, what is at stake in considering the outcome of Auden's enormous career—especially his overarching commitment, in the last twenty years of his life, to *"Bless what there is for being"* (CP 591), to "'look at / this world with a happy eye / but from a sober perspective'" (773), and to shun at all costs the temptations to which Prospero and Shelley succumbed. So let Heaney have the last word:

> Yet it is possible to grant the justice of Brodsky's praise and still regret the passing from Auden's poetry of an element of the uncanny, a trace of the Ralegh *frisson*, of the language's original "chief woe, world-sorrow." The price of an art that is so faithfully wedded to disenchantment and disintoxication, that seeks the heraldic shape beneath the rippling skin, that is impelled not only to lay down the law but to keep a civil tongue, the price of all this is a certain diminution of the language's autonomy, a not uncensorious training of its wilder shoots. (126)

Appendix

AUDEN AND MERTON AT THE MOVIES

The camera may
do justice to laughter, but must
degrade sorrow.

          —"I AM NOT A CAMERA"

When Hitler's armies invaded Poland in 1939, they brought camera crews with them. As past masters of the art of cinematic propaganda— it is sometimes forgotten that Leni Riefensthal's masterpiece, *Triumph of the Will,* had been made in 1934, only a year after Hitler assumed power—the Nazis understood that film equipment was nearly as vital to the Wehrmacht as tanks and guns. By November (less than two months after the invasion began, less than six weeks after its triumphant completion) a cinematic record of the Nazi victory was being shown in at least one theater in New York City. The filmmakers would have been interested to learn that their *Sieg im Polen* would soon have a profound effect on the lives of two literary intellectuals then living in New York. Each had complex ties to America and to Britain, ties which made his sense of citizenship problematic. One, the elder, was already famous in intellectual circles and considered by many to be the voice of his generation; the other's (more broadly based) fame would commence quite suddenly in another eight years. They were W. H. Auden and Thomas Merton. Humphrey Carpenter mentions Auden's viewing of the film in his *W. H. Auden*, as does Richard Davenport-Hines in his recent biography[1]; Michael Mott notes Merton's encounter with it (which he derives from Merton's own *Secular Journal*) in his *Seven Mountains of Thomas Merton*. But no one, to my knowledge, has recognized that the two men saw the same film; and thus no one has noted the peculiar similarities in their reactions to what they saw.

Of course, neither Auden nor Merton had to wait to see *Sieg im Polen* before being disturbed by the events of that September. Like many other Western intellectuals who did not believe that the Nazis would go so far, they were startled by the invasion. Auden was immediately prodded into writing one of his more famous poems, "September 1, 1939," an inquiry into causes: How could this have happened? What "has driven a culture mad"? Auden's answer was simple and direct: the countries that had placed such an enormous financial and moral burden on Germany with the Treaty of Versailles were responsible, and only pedantry could mask that responsibility:

> Accurate scholarship can
> Unearth the whole offense
> . . . . .
> I and the public know
> What all schoolchildren learn,
> Those to whom evil is done
> Do evil in return.   (EA 245)

Auden here presents, in essence, the argument of John Maynard Keynes's famous book *The Economic Consequences of the Peace* (1919), only simplified and moralized. The poem is distinctive in that it represents a rare moment of political confidence for the Auden of this period, whose commitment to the Left had been shaken by the excesses and abuses he saw on both sides in the Spanish Civil War.

In 1939 Auden had not yet returned to Christianity. Thomas Merton, on the other hand, had already made his later-to-be-famous entry into Catholicism—which may help to explain why, when he writes of the impending war, he blames, not the imperialist powers of Versailles, but himself:

> In my own mind [was] the recognition: "I myself am responsible for this. My sins have done this. Hitler is not the only one who has started this war: I have my share in it too . . ." It was a very sobering thought, and yet its deep and probing light by its very truth eased my soul a little. I made up my mind to go to confession and Communion on the first Friday of September. (*Seven* 248)

These reflections came in August 1939, just before the invasion of Poland, and were based on the stirrings in Europe already clearly evident; the confession Merton promised himself eventually came the day after the invasion and would prompt in him an excited determination to rely on and praise God in the midst of war: "She [the Church] was thanking Him [Christ] *in* the war, *in* the suffering; not for the war and for the suffering, but for His love which she knew was protecting her, and us, in this new crisis" (250).

Auden blames the Allies of World War I; Merton blames himself. Neither man fails to recognize the presence and activity of evil; but each is reluctant to equate evil's direct perpetrators with its source. The anti-Manicheanism of the rhetoric shared by Auden and Merton —the refusal to make "simplistic" distinctions between good and evil— is in some ways, and at some times, a noble and necessary stance; but in our cultural memory of the Second World War it is inevitably associated with Munich and the strategy of appeasement. What has been said so often since hardly needs repeating: that Hitler was no humanist, and furthermore that if many Westerners were not Manichean he, in his conviction that his every move was guided by what he called "Providence," surely was. (Which is why, many have argued, his fellow

Manichean Churchill was better qualified to fight him than the confidently humanistic businessman Neville Chamberlain.)

The rhetoric of Auden and Merton is, it should be noted, extreme even by anti-Manichean standards in its refusal to look at Hitler too closely, in its determination to shift moral attention to other, perhaps less frightening, less inexplicable, parties. The actions of a spirit rebellious against God, or of greedy and reckless Western Europeans, may be amenable to discipline, correction, rational argument; a "psychopathic god"—as Auden calls Hitler in the only such direct reference in "September 1, 1939"—most certainly will not be. Perhaps a subconscious recognition of this sheer chasm between Hitler and the moral ideals of humanism made both Auden and Merton particularly vulnerable to what they would see in *Sieg im Polen*.

Auden was the first of the two to see the film, soon after it arrived in New York that November. The theater was in Yorkville, a section of Manhattan then largely populated by people of German descent; German was often heard on the streets there. Not surprisingly, especially since the United States was not yet involved in the war, the moviegoers were quite sympathetic to the Nazi cause: since many of them had come to the United States during the economic crises that debilitated Germany in the 1920s, they knew what Hitler had done to restore German pride and economic and cultural stability.

But Auden, at least, was not prepared for the extremity of the viewers' reactions to this film. Whenever the Poles appeared on the screen—as prisoners, of course, in the hands of the Wehrmacht—the audience would shout, "Kill them! Kill them!" Auden was stunned. "There was no hypocrisy," he recalled many years later: these people were unashamed of their feelings and attempted to put no "civilized" face upon them. "I wondered, then, why I reacted as I did against this denial of every humanistic value." On what grounds did he have a right to demand—or even a reason to expect—a more "humanistic" response? His inability to answer this question, he explained, "brought me back to the Church" (Levy 42).[2]

The road back to the church began with this inquiry into the basis of value. There had to be some standard by which Hitler's wrongness —and that of his fanatical supporters in the American movie house— could be established. Auden soon began to look darkly on the whole intellectual tradition which had nourished and admired him throughout his career; he told Golo Mann (son of the novelist Thomas) that "the English intellectuals who now cry to Heaven against the evil incarnated in Hitler have no Heaven to cry to; they have nothing to offer and their prospects echo in empty space" (Spender, *Tribute* 102). Auden had clearly come a very long way in a very short time: we hear no more talk of the moral turpitude of the Treaty of Versailles. However, that talk is not replaced by "accurate scholarship," by a cultural or social explanation for the Nazi phenomenon. The "evil incarnated in Hitler" needs no (earthly) extrinsic provocation: cause and agent now are one, joined in the mystery of iniquity.

By October 1940 Auden had reentered the Christian church; but, if his recollections late in life are to be trusted, this was not the only consequence of his encounter with evil in Yorkville. His entire concept of the role and purpose of the poet, which had been in a state of confusion for some time, would soon be completely transformed. Through most of the thirties, Auden was of course a socially and politically active poet—in this regard, again, a leader of his generation. But, as I have suggested, the Spanish Civil War caused him to rethink his political stance; and now he was to withdraw from the political scene almost completely, in his work and his life, and to do so in a controversial fashion.[3]

Many Englishmen living abroad were returning to their homeland as the danger to it increased, but Auden steadfastly refused (under some pressure from friends, from the government, and from the press) even to visit. All attempts to get him involved in the war effort failed. However strong his sense of *cultural* Englishness might have been, his *political* ties to his country were weakening. (He would become an American citizen in 1946.) As his biographer Humphrey Carpenter says, "He does not seem to have questioned whether he had a moral duty to help, however trivially, in the fight against Hitler" (293). Though later in the war Auden would do some work in communications at the Pentagon, it is clear that from this time forward he strove to erase political consciousness from his poetry: he turned instead to poems of personal and social ethics, becoming—like the Roman Horace and the Frenchman Montaigne, who preceded him in this honorable occupation—a retiree from the battleground of history, devoted to the leisurely contemplation of ethical ideals. Auden's reflections on contemporary society after the conclusion of the war seem increasingly rarefied and general, the pronouncements of a sage, a "minor atlantic Goethe" (CP 693).

To say this is not to extol the *via activa* at the expense of the *via contemplativa*. Such "sageness" is a valid occupation indeed, and in Auden's case is often, one might say characteristically, redeemed by humility and self-deprecation. Furthermore, as Edward Mendelson has often and forcefully written, Auden's ethically reflective poems and essays form an important corrective to much modern poetry and poetics, for which the very notions of citizenship and responsibility are foreign; but his work nonetheless suggests a desire to preserve the permanence of ethics from the instability of politics. After the war Auden would increasingly often make a distinction between Arcadians and Utopians—those who look nostalgically to an ideal past versus those who strive for an ideal future—and would forcefully align himself with the former group; of his relation to his Utopian "Anti-type," he writes, "between my Eden and his New Jerusalem, no treaty is negotiable" (CP 638). Despite Auden's insistence in the same poem that both positions are necessary to the health of the human community, many will surely ask whether such an absolute division makes possible for all Arcadian Christians an avoidance of responsibility to the Kingdom of God, a pseudoethical excuse for political quietism.

In any event, nothing exemplifies the profound change in Auden's thinking more clearly than the history of his attitude toward "September 1, 1939." During the war, as Auden was working on his first edition of *Collected Poetry* (which would be published in 1945), he simply eliminated the stanza containing the poem's most famous line—one of the most memorable Auden would ever write: "We must love one another or die." This statement Auden later and repeatedly referred to as "a damned lie" (though it has been strenuously defended by even so morally sensitive a critic as Joseph Brodsky), and when, in 1955, an anthology editor especially fond of the original version of the poem pleaded for the inclusion of the excised stanza, Auden agreed only on condition that he change one word in the key line: "We must love one another *and* die" was the new reading. In the original line, and indeed in the whole poem, Auden came to perceive a naive faith in human goodness and in the inevitable triumph of love which, post-Yorkville, revolted him. His revulsion apparently intensified, for in later years (starting with the *Selected Poetry* he prepared for Faber in 1957 and Random House in 1958) he did remove the poem from all collections of his work that he oversaw. It was only restored by his literary executor Edward Mendelson in the *Selected Poems* of 1979, six years after the poet's death.[4]

In the 1971 interview in which he recalled his experience in Yorkville, he re-emphasized his "hate" for the poem, his conviction that it was a "lie." It was a lie because, as he said in his famous elegy for Yeats (written, it should be noted, *before* the invasion of Poland), "poetry makes nothing happen" (CP 248). He told the interviewer, "Nothing I wrote saved a single Jew from being gassed." Further, "It's perfectly all right to be an *engagé* writer as long as you don't think you're changing things. . . . The social and political history of Europe would be exactly the same if Dante and Shakespeare and Mozart had never lived" (Levy 42). And in several of his essays he quotes Shelley's claim that "poets are the unacknowledged legislators of the world" —which he regarded as "the silliest remark ever made about poets"— only to insist that such a statement is more properly applied to the Gestapo ("Squares" 27; DH 177). Legislation, which is to say political efficacy, can never belong to the true poet.

As any number of commentators—including Joseph Brodsky, whose essay on the poem is the best account of it likely to be written —have noted, Auden's dislike of the poem, even if well-founded, does not make it any less important. In the shrewd words of Nicholas

Jenkins: "Not since Andrew Marvell's 'Horatian Ode' had a poet made equivocation and doubt in the face of a major political event seem so representative a condition" (94).

Thomas Merton would not see *Sieg im Polen* until September of 1940, but he too saw it in Yorkville. Presumably the theater was celebrating the first anniversary of the successful invasion. The impact of the film on him is a little more difficult to assess: Merton, though a relentlessly autobiographical man, tends to obscure and oversimplify his own motives. *The Seven Storey Mountain* is about how God called him to be a monk; further inquiries into causation are to him mundane and irrelevant. Merton's persistent refusal to delve into difficult questions about his own decisions—a tendency which lasted until his death, through vast changes in conviction, practice and even, it sometimes appears, temperament—has again and again forced his biographers into a good deal of conjecture.

Only the chronology is clear. Merton was baptized into the Catholic Church in November of 1938, while a graduate student at Columbia. Almost immediately, it seems, he began considering the monastic life, but remained uncertain about his vocation for some time. He saw *Sieg im Polen* just before he left New York City to teach at St. Bonaventure, upstate. In Holy Week of 1941 he made a retreat at the Trappist Abbey of Gethsemane in Kentucky, to which he soon returned as a postulant. There, eventually, he would produce the work that would make him famous.

Did his viewing of the film have anything to do with his eventual decision to become a monk? Surely it was not as pivotal an event in his life as it was for Auden: Auden's inability to come to terms with the film and with the reaction to it seems to have caught him by surprise, while Merton was already aware that his life had become problematic. But seeing *Sieg im Polen* must have pushed Merton toward the monastic life he was already considering.

Merton recorded his trip to Yorkville in his journal. Unlike Auden, he saw nothing significant about the viewers of the film: "Everyone in Yorkville looked very peaceable except the waiters standing in the doors of the restaurants and bars" (*Secular* 130). Does such a comment suggest that Merton expected something other than peaceableness? Presumably the public's intensity had abated in the intervening year. Nor was he to note anything much about the Poles he saw on the screen. In fact, he was to find the film in general "nondescript," though in its repetitiveness "very nauseating and stupid." But one scene caught his attention, a scene focused on a portion of the conquering army, riding along in caissons:

> Suddenly one man got in the eye of the camera, and gave back the straightest and fiercest and most resentful look I ever saw. Great rings surrounded his eyes which were full of exhaustion, pain and protest. And he kept staring, turning his head and fixing his eyes on the camera as he went by demanding to be seen as a person, and not as the rest of the cattle. The censors should have cut him out, because he succeeded. (128)

(We may be sure that neither Auden nor Merton lacked sympathy for the nations oppressed by the Nazi armies; but it is interesting that for both of them the first impulse is to identify and sympathize with the German people, to see them as the first victims.)

Michael Mott, Merton's best biographer, suggests that the image of this man stayed with Merton when, less than a year later, he faced some important decisions. The next March, at almost exactly the same time that he received word that the Abbey of Gethsemane would allow him to make a retreat there during Holy Week, he received the customary "Greetings" from the draft board. In his journal he records that, on receiving this notice, "I got all my notions together about war, and said them, briefly, all at once . . . I mean I made out my reasons for being a partial Conscientious Objector, for asking for non-combatant service, so as not to have to kill men made in the image of God when it is possible to obey the law (as I must) by serving the wounded and saving lives" (quoted in Mott 169). It is not difficult to imagine that Merton had in mind the face of that lone soldier when he wrote of those "men made in the image of God."

Conscientious objection marked, for Merton, only a moral and ethical way-station. It is perfectly obvious that moral dilemmas such as this one contributed to Merton's eventual choice of the monastic life: there he could pray for the world single-mindedly, without the distractions and confusions the political world offered to the ordinary person.[5] The Abbey of Gethsemane became Merton's equivalent for Auden's less spectacular, and apparently less drastic, retirement. Merton withdrew to a specific physical place, Auden only to an intellectual position; but the monk and the sage equally desired an escape from the dilemmas of politics and into the relative directness and simplicity of moral contemplation.

Yet it must be said that, after a few years, Merton became dissatisfied in some ways with the monastic answer: he felt ever more strongly, as the years wore on, the call to political activism from within the monastery. Merton eventually accomplished a transformation of his career that (as his biographers and critics have noted) is odd and possibly self-contradictory: he arranged to become a hermit, living alone in a small cottage some distance from the Abbey proper (though still on the Abbey's property) in a way not normally approved of by his profoundly communal Cistercian order; but at the same time he grew increasingly involved with political issues, and would reach his greatest fame in the 1960s as an activist in the peace and civil rights movements. As he moved away from communion with his fellow monks, he seems to have found a new communion with devotees of social and political causes, who welcomed him as a strong ally and even a leader.

Perhaps in this latter part of his career Merton had reached an acceptable compromise: the moral satisfaction of being politically active coupled with the security, the refuge, of the monastery. It is as though Merton's experience with World War II—including, perhaps as an important component, his visit to the theater in Yorkville— provoked a flight from the political world that he later regretted but could not bring himself to reverse. Despite many threats to leave the monastery, Merton never did so, and some critics doubt whether returning to public life was ever a real possibility for him. But did this compromise with politics mean, ultimately, the abdication of full responsibility for his actions, the avoidance of genuine commitment?

What accounts for the power—in the life of at least one of these men, a catalytic power—of *Sieg im Polen*? Perhaps the shocking novelty of the cinematic presentation of war played a part. One must remember the near-hysterical response of the crowd the night Auden saw the film. It has been suggested that at this time reactions to filmed images of the "real," especially the violently real, had not yet been assimilated to daily experience: those images had not yet become routinized, as they would in the rest of the war. Because Auden's poetry and Merton's piety could provide no control over the images which confronted them, they refined and strengthened their poetic and devotional lives at the expense of direct contact with the suffering world.

But these reactions are not just a testimony to the power of film; they are, more importantly, an index into the failure of many modern intellectuals to unite art or religion with political action. In fact, the avenues of response Auden and Merton chose are surely admirable in comparison with the confused inaction demonstrated by so many of their contemporaries: at least these two understood that the situation demanded serious measures. Moreover, the disturbing political stances taken by so many modernist writers, and the possibility (in some critical circles an *idée reçue*) that authoritarian politics is logically associated with certain aspects of the modernist aesthetic, might encourage one to prefer as a lesser evil intellectual inconsistency, that severance of art and religion from the political world at issue here. The careers of Pound and Eliot, Joyce and Yeats (among many others), with their apparent embrace of authoritarianism, present precisely the kinds of embarrassments that Auden and Merton foresee and are almost desperate to avoid; thus their peculiar but strategic withdrawals from the public arena.

In reply to my argument, Auden could point to the ethical commitment of his later poetry; but this is to avoid recognizing that the consistently universal and personal emphases of his ethics make it in effect politically inapplicable. Merton could point to the political commitment of his later years; but as I have already noted, the abbey provided a kind of safety net for him, a refuge from the perils and confusions of the fully committed political life. For both of these writers, *Sieg im Polen* provided an impetus: encountering the Nazis' proud demonstration of military accomplishment, they discovered their own participation in the moral confusion of the age. In another revealing passage from "September 1, 1939," Auden suggested that the whole Western world was seeking reassuring habits, delusive comforts, in order

> To make this fort assume
> The furniture of home;
> Lest we should see where we are,
> Lost in a haunted wood,
> Children afraid of the night
> Who have never been happy or good.   (EA 246)

So each of these two frightened children sought a new life: Auden the lonely sage, Merton the activist monk. From the risks of commitment to the political world, they fled—or were forced—into the haven of strictly personal ethics, where they could assume their moral stances without fear of compromise or confusion.

Notes

INTRODUCTION

1. For Jarrell's anti-Auden arguments, see chapter 4 below.

2. The most thorough and thoughtful investigation of Auden's reputation in the thirties—was it really as high as Samuel Hynes's famous title *The Auden Generation* suggests?—is Valentine Cunningham's in his second chapter, "Vin Rouge Audenaire?" Cunningham's answer is, more or less, yes.

Even Auden's father seems to have thought him something of a traitor to his fame and influence, writing (or so Auden himself said in his wounded reply, only recently discovered) that he wanted his son to be "the mouthpiece of an epoch." Auden explained that if a poet "wants to be the mouthpiece of his age, as every writer does, it must be the last thing he thinks about" (quoted in Jenkins 92).

3. Auden wrote to Monroe Spears in 1963: "You're right, of course, about my daydream of a large audience, but I cannot tell you how embarrassed and distressed I felt during those years in the Thirties when I was 'in fashion.' I knew the popularity had nothing to do with any real value my work might have and that I should, very justly, have to pay for it later" (Berg Collection).

4. In light of this argument it is worth noting that in 1945, when Auden published his *Collected Poetry* for the first time, he arranged the poems in alphabetical order by title. In a 1951 letter to Stephen Spender he explained his intentions: "My reason for doing that was not to pretend that I have gone through no historical change, but because there are so very few readers who can be trusted to approach one's poems without a preconceived notion of what that development has been, I wanted to test ['catch out' deleted] the reader who believes that my earliest poems are the best; eg make him read a poem and then guess its date" (Bucknell and Jenkins, *Map* 87). In 1965, returning to the task of collection, he overcame his desire *épater les lecteurs* and provided a historical framework for the poems. He also gave a different explanation for the curious organization of the 1945 edition: "This may have been a silly thing to do, but I had a reason. At the age of thirty-seven I was still too young to have any sure

sense of the direction in which I was moving, and I did not wish critics to waste their time, and mislead readers, making guesses about it which would almost certainly turn out to be wrong. To-day, nearing sixty, I believe that I know myself and my poetic intentions better and, if anybody wants to look at my writings from an historical perspective, I have no objection" (CP xxv). I do not know when Auden developed the distinction between major and minor artists that he uses in reference to Stravinsky (those words were written in 1971), but it seems likely that his decision to organize his work chronologically was a mark of his claim to being an artist of the first rank.

As early as 1940, in another letter to Spender, Auden was starting to think of his work, and his character, as finding their proper form only over the long haul: "People imagine that I absorb things easily and quickly: this is true only in the most superficial way. On the contrary I am really someone who has to grow very slowly; I develop slower than most people" (Bucknell and Jenkins, *Map* 72).

CHAPTER 1: CHANGE

1. Stan Smith believes that Auden, more or less throughout his career, held just such a view (12). I find this an exaggeration, but a useful one in that it confirms my point that Auden was never, despite his erstwhile enthusiasm for Kierkegaard, as much of an existentialist as many critics have portrayed him to be.

2. Fish has recently been at some pains to distinguish himself from Rorty, but chiefly on the question of what, to borrow a phrase from Rorty, the consequences of pragmatism are (*There's* 214–19). Fish clearly places himself in the "pragmatist camp" (215), though he tends to prefer the word "localist" (298).

3. For a more detailed exploration of this point, see my essay "Unnatural Practices."

4. One of the few direct references to Pascal in *The Prolific and the Devourer* is another of Auden's wonderfully ambiguous evaluations:

> I feel about Pascal as Pascal felt about Montaigne. Of all the dualists he is incomparably the noblest and most seductive. Like most of us he exalted the faculty he lacked over the faculty he possessed, the heart over the reason, and fashioned an image out of his opposite. . . .
>
> By all appearances he should have been damned, but he was saved, and saved not as he thought by his heart but by his reason, for it was his reason that told him that his heart was corrupt and that therefore the love of human beings was not for him. (47–48)

CHAPTER 2: THE CRITIQUE OF ROMANTICISM

1. "As to his undergraduate reading in poetry, he soon decided that Wordsworth was 'a most bleak old bore'. Indeed the Romantics in general did not appeal to him, and he said he had 'no use' for Keats or Shelley" (Carpenter 54). To be fair, it must be admitted that few undergraduates of any stripe care for Wordsworth, but Auden's dislike of him would persist: one of the reasons he gave for writing his "Letter to Lord Byron" was that Byron didn't care for Wordsworth (Carpenter 199).

For another view of Auden's relation to Romanticism, see Blair, chapter 1. Also see, for an argument whose lines in some ways anticipate my own, Callan's chapter 10, "Disenchantment with Yeats."

2. Even professional critics of Romanticism, as Jerome McGann has pointed out, tend to emphasize the "uniformities" of Romanticism at the expense of the "differentials" (107). Interestingly, McGann's attempt to discriminate among some of the varieties and phases of Romanticism leads him to formulations quite close, as we shall see, to those of Auden. For instance, his contrast between Wordsworth's idealization of the past (81–92) and Shelley's status as a "cureless idealist . . . a meliorist, a futurist, an escapist with a vaporous style to match his airy thoughts and dreams" (116) echoes Caliban's distinction in *The Sea and the Mirror*, as described later in this chapter, between those who turn to him for help and those who turn to Ariel.

3. Interestingly, the psychomachic interpretation of the play is a Romantic invention; it probably originates with A. W. Schlegel.

4. As Edward Callan has pointed out (172), this critique of "halfness" is characteristic of Auden's reflections on Romanticism in this period. In "New Year Letter" he refers to "The either-ors, the mongrel halves, / Who find truth in a mirror" (CP 220), and in his notes to the poem glosses these lines: "i.e., the impatient romantics. (Definition of Romanticism: unawareness of the Dialectic.)" (*Double* 115). Auden then goes on, in the note, to distinguish between these "impatient romantics" and the "lazy Romantics"—we may see Shelley and Wordsworth behind these categories. It is perhaps notable that, though (as I will later argue) Auden had more temperamental sympathy with the "lazy romantics," he thought that the "impatient romantic sees more clearly"—but only sees half the picture and, believing his or her vision to be whole, is thereby particularly dangerous. A few lines later in the "Letter" Auden celebrates "the gift of double focus," the ability to see both sides of a paradox, and not to complete one's partial vision only by looking in a mirror.

We see in these passages a fairly early instance of Auden's fascination with narcissism, to which he felt himself (as a homosexual and an "endomorph") doubly subject. Another example may be found in the first of the columns he wrote for *Commonweal* in 1942 under the name Didymus (see Deedy 21–24). This column reappears, in a slightly different version, as the first part of the essay "Hic et Ille" (DH 93–106).

5. A common assumption, of course, is that one's childhood was so fine because the world as a whole was better and more pure then; see Raymond Williams's brilliant analysis of this topos in *The Country and the City*: he traces the beckoning specter of "the organic community of old England" all the way back past More's *Utopia* (chapter 2). See also Frank Kermode's critique of the quest for an age of unified sensibility in the last chapter of *Romantic Image*.

6. Cf. Gerald Graff's argument: "The poet as hypersensitive weakling and the poet as prophet (or revolutionary) . . . frequently merge in the same figure" (16).

In treating Auden's view of Shelley, I do not question it; but it should be noted that the modernist distaste for Shelley has been vigorously contested in recent years, most notably by Harold Bloom and Jonathan Culler.

7. The invocation of Dante here is not arbitrary. The notebooks Auden used in writing this poem, and a chart he prepared at the same time for a class he taught at Swarthmore called "Romanticism from Rousseau to Hitler," indicate that he was thinking along just these lines. In that chart he showed two roads leading from the Fall of Man which correspond to the two fates outlined by Caliban: the first, "the Hell of the Pure Deed," is the Wordsworthian Inferno; the second, "the Hell of the Pure Word," is that of Shelley. Auden's image for the first is the forest, for the second the desert—images which he would later develop in *The Enchafèd Flood*. See Spears 247–49.

8. If Romanticism is the natural extension of Protestantism—as Auden seems to have believed—it is interesting that in the notes to "New Year Letter" Auden cites Paul Tillich's *Interpretation of History*, which gives a specifically Protestant take on the necessity of rejecting the Romantic means of escape from historical contingency: "The fundamental Protestant attitude is to stand in nature, taking upon oneself the inevitable reality; not to flee from it, either into the world of ideal forms or into the related world of super-nature, but to make decisions in concrete reality. Here the subject has no possibility of an absolute position. It cannot go out of the sphere of decision. Every part of its nature is affected by these contradictions" (quoted in *Double* 132).

9. Justin Repogle has argued that Caliban's description is not of two strains of Romanticism, but rather of Kierkegaard's aesthetic and ethical stages—in which case the alternative is simple: the religious. But as influential as Kierkegaard was over Auden at this point in the poet's career, I cannot see his categories at work in this section of the poem (though in Prospero's opening monologue Kierkegaard is echoed repeatedly): the two groups who hope to be rescued from their historical lives are equally aesthetic in their concerns, and neither shows the

slightest interest in ethical reflection. Conversely, the references to Romanticism are too central to be neglected.

10. From the last stanza of "Les Phares":

> Car c'est vraiment, Seigneur, le meilleur témoignage
> Que nous puissions donner de notre dignité
> Que cet ardent sanglot qui roule d'âge en âge
> Et vient mourir au bord de votre éternité! (Baudelaire 196)

> This, O Lord, is the best evidence
> that we can offer of our dignity,
> this sob that swells from age to age and dies
> out on the shore of Your eternity! (18)

11. A poem in which Auden treats this theme, and in a tone that seems to oscillate between sympathetic critique and utter scorn, is "Voltaire at Ferney" (1939):

> So, like a sentinel, he could not sleep. The night was full of wrong,
> Earthquakes and executions. Soon he would be dead,
> And still all over Europe stood the horrible nurses
> Itching to boil their children. Only his verses
> Perhaps could stop them: He must go on working. Overhead
> The uncomplaining stars composed their lucid song. (CP 251)

Even if the hope of ending cruelty by the power of poetry is a ludicrous one, one feels that Auden has a certain respect for Voltaire's determination to keep working. It beats making sonorous pronouncements about who the legislators of the world might be.

12. In the "Commentary" to "In Time of War," written in 1938, Auden speaks of the need for "gratitude to the Invisible College of the Humble, / Who through the ages have accomplished everything essential" (EA 268). The matter of humility will be taken up again and in more detail in the next chapter.

13. Cf. Ricoeur, *Freud and Philosophy*: "The movement by which man empties himself into transcendence is secondary as compared to the movement by which he grasps hold of the Wholly Other in order to objectify and make use of it. . . .

> This objectifying process is the origin both of metaphysics
> and of religion: metaphysics makes God into a supreme being;
> and religion treats the sacred as a new sphere of objects, insti-
> tutions, and powers within the world of immanence. . . .
> Henceforward there are sacred *objects* and not merely *signs* of
> the sacred; sacred objects in addition to the world of culture.
> This [is a] diabolic transformation. . . . (529–30)

---

14. See the fuller treatment of this question (including Johnson's response) in chapter 3, below.

15. See the analyses of this aspect of Auden's career in McDiarmid, *Saving*, especially chapter 1, and Scott, chapter 3, as well as Mendelson passim.

16. But see Mendelson: "The cold fury that marked Auden's attacks on Shelley emerged almost certainly from his recognition of the dangerous degree of sympathy which in fact he held for Shelley's purposes and style. Eliot also dismissed Shelley, but then Eliot could not have sounded like Shelley if he tried. Auden felt tempted to sound very much like him indeed" (201). I wish Mendelson had provided some evidence to support this claim, for it seems to me that Auden had a loathing of Shellyan pretension virtually from the beginning of his career—despite, or perhaps because of, his admirers' attempts to push him into the role of an unacknowledged legislator.

On Auden's relations to Wordsworth in his early career, see Mendelson's acute reading of the 1930 poem "This lunar beauty" (82–83).

17. It is interesting that in formulating the Eden–New Jerusalem polarity, key to the later Auden's cultural hermeneutics, he would recur to a polarity he had found essential when he was on the verge of becoming a Christian. Auden's important reflections on the nature of Eden may be found in DH 6–7 and, especially, 409–15.

18. See also his hopeful comment about the future of poetry in the introduction to the fifth volume of the anthology of English-language poetry that he and Norman Holmes Pearson edited: "What will happen is anyone's guess. Perhaps history is forcing the intellectual, whether scientist or artist, into a new conception of himself as neither the respectable bard nor the anarchic aesthete, but as a member of the Loyal Opposition, defending, not for his sake only but for all, the inalienable rights of the individual person against encroachment by an overzealous government, with which, nevertheless, even though the latter deny it, he has a bond, their common love for the Just City" (xxv).

19. My attention was called to this passage by Mendelson; see his analysis of its importance (xiii–xiv). Auden tells the same story elsewhere (DH 102).

CHAPTER 3: THE HORATIANS

1. This ambivalence toward Yeats, so evident in the famous elegy (CP 247) and in the prose piece written at almost the same time, "The Public v. the Late Mr. William Butler Yeats" (EA 389), veers toward utter repudiation in the character of Mittenhofer, the repulsive poet of Auden and Kallman's libretto for *Elegy for Young Lovers*, whom they admittedly modeled on Yeats (see L 663). Later, in a 1964 letter to Stephen Spender, Auden would call Yeats his "devil of inauthenticity" (Carpenter 416), suggesting that his own reaction to Yeats was so strong,

and the temptations which Yeats as a poetic model presented him with so great, that he could not be fair in his comments about Yeats. It is worth noting, however, that, according to Humphrey Carpenter, Auden's house in Kirchstetten had on its walls "only three pictures of note: drawings of Stravinsky and Richard Strauss, and an Augustus John etching of Yeats" (390). But it is also worth noting that, in the section of "Thanksgiving for a Habitat" in which he describes his living room ("The Common Life") he mentions only "the portrayed regards of Strauss and Stravinsky" (CP 715)!

See Callan's chapter 10, "Disenchantment with Yeats" (143–62), and Stan Smith's essay, "Persuasions to Rejoice: Auden's Oedipal Dialogues with W. B. Yeats," in Bucknell and Jenkins, *Language* (155–64).

2. See "William Blake and His Illustrations to the *Divine Comedy*," in *Essays and Introductions* (116–45).

3. Auden's claim to a connection may have been nothing more than an attempt to identify himself as, like Langland, a "poet of the People"; though he did point out to Alan Ansen that the poem Ansen knew as "Speech from a Play" (which appeared in *New Verse* in February 1935) "is in the Piers Plowman kind of alliterative" (51–52). The "play" of the poem's title is *The Chase*; see *Plays* 147–49. Auden also uses a similar form in *The Age of Anxiety*, his most allegorical work.

4. On Tolkien's heresy in making the Orcs damned as a species, see the letter to Peter Salus of 11 August 1964 (Berg Collection). On Williams's limitations, especially as a writer of fiction, see Auden's introduction to the 1956 Meridian edition of Williams's *Descent of the Dove*. On Hardy: "He was a good poet, perhaps a great one, but not *too* good. Much as I loved him, even I could see that his diction was often clumsy and forced and that a lot of his poems were plain bad. This gave me hope where a flawless poet might have made me despair" (DH 38).

On Auden's changing attitudes toward Kierkegaard, see especially his 1968 review of the English edition of Kierkegaard's *Journals and Papers*, which is in essence an attempt to make amends for the virtually uncritical enthusiasm for Kierkegaard which he had exhibited in the early forties (F&A 182–97; that early enthusiasm is recorded in the immediately previous selection in the same book).

5. As far as I know, the only response Auden ever made to Randall Jarrell's vituperation was a comment to Alan Ansen: "Jarrell is really just trying to flout Papa." But even this is followed by a softening remark: "Of course, he is really quite a good man; that's what makes his mistakes so irritating" (19). These comments, which Ansen dates 15 January 1947, seem to be in response to Jarrell's essay "Freud to Paul: the Stages of Auden's Ideology," which first appeared in *Partisan Review* 12 (fall 1945). Golo Mann, who lived with Auden when he was a particularly controversial figure because of his refusal to return to England for the war, was struck by Auden's indifference towards attacks on his poetry and character (Spender, *Tribute* 112).

For a thorough account of the Auden-Jarrell relationship, see Ian Sansom's "Flouting Papa," in Bucknell and Jenkins, *In Solitude* 273–88.

6. I cite these judgments from Weinbrot (3); for an excellent analysis of this peculiar history of historical claims, disclaims, and counter-claims, see Weinbrot passim, but especially the introduction (on Dryden's "Discourse") and chapter 2, on Horace and Caesar Augustus.

7. For a vivid and stimulating account of the traditions of "civic leisure" and "retired leisure," which has influenced my thinking about the issues raised in this chapter and the next, see O'Loughlin; his third chapter treats largely of Horace.

8. The first direct reference to Horace in Auden's poetry, as far as I can see, comes in "Love Letter" (a poem originally published in a Kenyon College literary magazine and reprinted in Bucknell and Jenkins, *Language* [42]) and is rather negative: "the bland Horatian life of culture and wines." Auden liked that line; see also the poem "Christmas 1940": "The bland Horatian life of friends and wine" (EA 460).

9. If there is a literary genre in the modern world which is characteristically Horatian, it is the essay. In fact, many of the great exponents of the familiar essay in the English tradition—especially Lamb and Hazlitt—likely would have been in an earlier generation Horatian poets rather than prose writers. Conversely, many of the lengthy discursive and meditative poems of, say, William Cowper would almost certainly have been essays had he lived half a century later.

In this context a judgment from Philip Larkin's review of Auden's *Homage to Clio* (referred to in this book's introduction) may be worth quoting. Of poems like "In Praise of Limestone," "Homage to Clio," and "Goodbye to the Mezzogiorno," Larkin writes, "He has begun to produce a kind of long reflective poem in a stabilized tone in which every facet of his subject is exhibited at leisure. . . . These poems are agreeable and ingenious essays, more closely directed than his earlier excursions such as 'August for the people' or 'Here on the cropped grass,' but their poetic pressure is not high—nor, indeed, is it intended to be" (126–27).

10. Compare the similar argument of Dr. Johnson in his life of Waller: "Let no pious ear be offended if I advance, in opposition to many authorities, that poetical devotion cannot much please. . . . Contemplative piety, or the intercourse between God and the human soul, cannot be poetical. Man admitted to implore the mercy of his Creator, and plead the merits of his Redeemer, is already in a higher state than poetry can confer. . . . All that pious verse can do is to help the memory, and delight the ear, and for these purposes it may be very useful; but it supplies nothing to the mind. The ideas of Christian theology are too simple for eloquence, too sacred for fiction, and too majestic for ornament; to recommend them by tropes and figures, is to magnify by a concave mirror the sidereal hemisphere" (*Lives* I. 291). Also Johnson's life of Watts (III: 310).

11. A wonderfully ambivalent aside in the notes to "New Year Letter": "A poet's prayer 'Lord, teach me to write so well, that I shall no longer want to'" (*Double* 86).

12. His description, referred to in chapter 2, of the Eden/New Jerusalem, Arcadian/Utopian polarity in "Dingley Dell and the Fleet" illustrates this point. When Auden says that the motto of the New Jerusalem is "In His will is our peace" (DH 409), he gives to his opponents the famous words of Piccarda the nun in the third canto of Dante's *Paradiso* (*"En la sua volontade è nostra pace"*); he takes for himself and his fellow Arcadians the entire constitution of Rabelais's Edenic Abbey of Thélème ("Do what thou wilt is here the law"). Each model draws equally on Christian tradition. Moreover, it is likely that both Auden and Rabelais intentionally echo the words of Virgil in Dante's *Purgatorio*, who tells the pilgrim Dante, when he has passed through each level of Purgatory and is about to enter the Earthly Paradise, or Eden, that he would be in error not to heed his newly and fully purified will (the concluding lines of canto 29). We shall see Piccarda again in chapter 5.

13. As quoted by his nephew Czeslaw Milosz (*Witness* 26ff.). Interestingly, Seamus Heaney uses the same phrase in reference to Auden, near the end of an essay that generally (though with qualifications) laments Auden's abandonment of his early voices and stances: "His responsibility towards the human family became intensely and commendably strong and the magnificently sane, meditative, judicial poems of the 1940s, 1950s and 1960s were the result" (127).

CHAPTER 4: LOCAL CULTURE

1. For another reading of "New Year Letter" as a key transitional poem, see Hynes, "Voice."

2. There is reason to think that Auden had this poem in mind when he was writing "New Year Letter." While the later poem describes, as noted above, the rising of the sun with its "neutral" and uncomprehending vision of the world below, "A Summer Night" describes the rising of the moon in very similar terms:

> She climbs the European sky;
> Churches and power stations lie
>   Alike among earth's fixtures:
> Into the galleries she peers,
> And blankly as an orphan stares
>   Upon the marvellous pictures.
>
> To gravity attentive, she
> Can notice nothing here.... (EA 137)

This curious parallel can be explained, perhaps, by Auden's habit in the early 1940s (noted by Edward Mendelson [SP xiv]) of returning not only to the themes of his earlier work but also to its genres and, as it were, rewriting his career.

3. "Discourse on the Nature and Offices of Friendship," from the 1847 edition of Taylor's *Works* as quoted by Meilaender 1. I am also indebted to Meilaender for the comment by Dr. Johnson which follows.

4. Perhaps the clearest illustration of this rejection comes in a 1941 letter to Stephen Spender in which he says, among other things, "I have absolutely no patience with Pacifism as a political movement" (Bucknell and Jenkins, *Map* 77). Two years earlier, in *The Prolific and the Devourer*, he had said "if by pacifism you mean simply the refusal to bear arms, I have very little use for it"; but he had also said that "my position"—by which I think he means, his position on the social role of the artist—"forbids me to act as a combatant in any war" (87).

5. Quoted by Jarrell; Auden's review appeared in the *New York Times*, 12 November 1944.

6. Reinhold Niebuhr, in *The Nature and Destiny of Man*, claims that this can indeed happen to certain kinds of radical Protestants: "Theologies, such as that of Barth, which threaten to destroy all relative moral judgments by their exclusive emphasis upon the ultimate religious fact of the sinfulness of all men, are rightly suspected of imperilling relative moral achievements of history" (I:220). In this case Auden clearly comes down on Niebuhr's side—he called Niebuhr's book "the most lucid and balanced statement of orthodox Protestantism we are likely to see for a long time" ("Means" 766)—as opposed to Barth's.

7. Auden later changed the word "voluntary" to "ordinary" (CP 320), which seems to blunt the force of the poem's conclusion. The same idea appears in the penultimate line of the last sonnet in "In Time of War": "We live in freedom by necessity" (EA 262). In "New Year Letter" also it appears in overtly paradoxical form:

> How grandly would our virtues bloom
> In a more conscionable dust
> Where Freedom dwells because it must,
> Necessity because it can. . . . (CP 240)

In his Notes to the poem Auden writes, "for this quotation, and for the source of many ideas in this poem, v. *The Descent of the Dove* by Charles Williams" (*Double* 153). In the ninety pages of notes to this poem, this tribute is unique. It is precisely analogous to the credit Eliot gives, in his notes to *The Waste Land*— on which Auden modeled his practice of providing an account of sources and quotations—to Jessie Weston's *From Ritual to Romance* (see *Collected* 70). In his book Williams says of Kierkegaard that "he co-ordinated experiences in a new manner; say, using the old word, that he caused alien and opposite experiences to co-inhere" (212). "Co-inherence" is the key term in Williams's peculiar theology; it means (generally speaking) to live one another's sufferings, to bear one another's burdens, to enjoy one another's joys, and to do all this "in Christ" (se Cavaliero passim for a full explanation); in genuine co-inherence the barriers of selfhood are dissolved, distinctions among persons as well as between any one person and God are lost. Williams says that the motto of his book is "This also is Thou; neither is this Thou" (viii). Williams's emphasis on what Auden believed to be a dialectical reconciliation of opposites provided for Auden, as he moved closer to Christian orthodoxy, a way of getting beyond the polarities which had come to dominate his thinking, especially in writing *The Prolific and the Devourer*. I would contend that "New Year Letter," as Auden's last major work before his conversion, is a final attempt to strike a balance between the conceptual world of his early poetry and the Christianity that he was increasingly drawn to. Interestingly, once Auden committed himself to Christianity he became more aware of Williams's limitations and eccentricities, though he never ceased to admire him.

On Auden's propensity for binary oppositions see Blair 73–76. We will return to the freedom/necessity pair in the afterword.

8. Larkin's 1960 review of *Homage to Clio* zeroes in nicely on this point. The early Auden, says Larkin, was intimately and profoundly connected to his cultural universe: "Few poets since Pope"—since Pope!—"have been so committed to their period" (124). In Larkin's view this commitment was Auden's chief source of poetic strength. Larkin therefore concludes that Auden could only sustain poetic strength by cultivating an equal attachment to his new homeland, America, and that, having failed to achieve such attachment, he was ruined as a poet. "Auden has not, in fact, gone in the direction one hoped: he has not adopted America or taken root, but has pursued an individual and cosmopolitan path which has precluded the kind of identification that seemed so much a part of his previous success" (127). This argument holds if and only if Larkin is right in assuming—and surely it is a natural assumption—that one who is "cosmopolitan" must also be "individual." What Auden hopes is that this equation does not hold.

9. A lighter version of this point comes in "Thanksgiving for a Habitat," where Auden describes his Austrian home as a kind of democracy-in-nature:

> I, a transplant
>
> from overseas, at last am dominant
>   over three acres and a blooming
> conurbation of country lives, few of whom
>   I shall ever meet, and with fewer

converse. Linnaeus recoiled from the Amphibia
　　as a naked gruesome rabble,
Arachnids give me the shudders, but fools
　　who deface their emblem of guilt

are germane to Hitler: the race of spiders
should be allowed their webs. (CP 689–90)

10. Auden never gave in completely to this tendency, and certainly did not always feel that friends should be kept at a distance. Again in "Thanksgiving for a Habitat," a poem called "For Friends Only" and dedicated to John and Teckla Clark, describes the Austrian house's guest room and begins thus:

Ours yet not ours, being set apart
As a shrine to friendship,
Empty and silent most of the year,
This room awaits from you
What you alone, as visitor, can bring,
A weekend of personal life. (CP 706)

But in light of the comments to MacNeice, a later stanza may be thought to have a double meaning:

Distance and duties divide us,
　　but absence will not seem an evil
If it make our re-meeting
A real occasion. (707)

CHAPTER 5: EROS AND AGAPE

1. Mendelson also provides the best account, by far, of Auden's complex and shifting thought about love in the years preceding his move to America: see *Early*, especially chapters 8 and 10.

2. Critics have often speculated on who "the inconstant ones" are. Anthony Hecht, for instance, suggests three possibilities: 1) homosexuals; 2) northern European tourists in the Mediterranean (Auden wrote the poem while visiting Italy, where he later came to spend his summers, in 1948); and 3) "all mortals" (305–6). The latter suggestion cannot be right, since the inconstant who prefer limestone are contrasted, in the poem, with very different classes of people associated with other stones and other landscapes. Of the other two possibilities the former seems most likely, since Auden frequently wrote, especially in letters, that the great difficulty of gay life derives from a tendency toward promiscuity coupled with a deep need for fidelity. Alan Ansen relates this comment: "Sexual fidelity is

more important in a homosexual relationship than in any other. In other relationships there are a variety of ties. But here, fidelity is the only bond" (81).

Nevertheless, I think the essential point of the poem is missed if inconstancy is confined to any one particular group that can be defined according to any terms other than inconstancy itself: my assumption, as will be evident, is that inconstancy in this poem is primarily a matter of spiritual temperament; such a temperament may produce various consequences in the sexual and ethical lives of the inconstant but is of interest to Auden chiefly in its original spiritual form.

3. When the study of "imagery" comes into fashion again, some acute critic should take a careful look at the way the moon appears in Auden's poetry: from the early transient "lunar beauty" to the indifferent and vacuous observer of the world in "A Summer Night" to the combination of "Goddess" and "bunch of barren craters" in the "Nocturne" of 1951 (CP 586).

4. Mendelson dates this poem "? Autumn 1940." Certain phrases and ideas in the poem seem to echo Denis de Rougemont's Love in the Western World, Auden's review of which appeared in the Nation in June 1941. The archetypes of extravagant (in the etymological sense) love that Auden chooses in this poem—and which he employs in the review—remind us that he was also, at this time, a recent convert (via Chester Kallman) to the joys of opera, the artistic medium which would for the rest of his life be central to his thinking about love and its aesthetic representations, as we shall see later in this chapter.

5. In a Christmas 1941 letter to Chester, discussed more fully below, Auden wrote, "on account of you, I have been, in intention and almost in act, a murderer" (Farnan 66). Auden often in later years made oblique reference to this experience—for example, in this passage from an account of the events surrounding his return to Christianity: "I was forced to know in person what it is like to feel oneself in the prey of demonic powers, in both the Greek and the Christian sense, stripped of self-control and self-respect, behaving like a ham actor in a Strindberg play" (Modern 41).

6. See also these aphoristic lines from "Thanksgiving for a Habitat": "Our bodies cannot love: / But, without one, / What works of Love could we do?" (CP 713) And in 1964 Auden would write, "Whatever else is asserted by the doctrine of the resurrection of the body, it asserts the sacred importance of the body" (F&A 68).

7. On Auden's "my-mother-made-me-a-homosexual" theory, see Carpenter 12, 258, etc.; also Mendelson, Early 59. In light of Auden's fascination with the Tristan and Isolde relationship, this story is interesting: "My mother," Auden wrote, "could be very odd indeed. When I was eight years old, she taught me the words and music of the love-potion scene in Tristan, and we used to sing it together" (F&A 501). This story is confirmed by his older brother John Auden (Spender, Tribute 27).

8. Auden did not think that heterosexuals *only* were subject to the idolatry of eros: in fact, he claimed that "the instances in real life which conform most closely to the original pattern of both myths are not, in either case, heterosexual; the Tristan and Isolde one actually meets are a Lesbian couple, the Don Juan a pederast" (F&A 25). It is interesting, though, that Auden specifies a *lesbian* Tristan and Isolde, implying by this specification that gay males are less likely to incarnate that myth.

9. On the very limited role Luther gives to natural theology, see Althaus, chapters 2 and 3. Barth's attitude toward natural theology is neatly summed up in the title of a little book he wrote in response to Emil Brunner's limited defense of natural theology: *Nein*. It is also noteworthy, given Auden's reading in the years leading up to his return to Christianity, that Blake too is famous for declaring (at the outset of his career) that "THERE is NO natural religion" (1).

But only a few years after his conversion, in 1950, Auden would write self-critically of the dangers of "a Barthian exaggeration of God's transcendence" (*Religion* 25).

10. Auden is careful to separate the Platonic and Dantean strands of this tradition, a separation which indicates the care with which he thought about it:

> The two most serious attempts to analyze the Vision of Eros and give it theological significance are Plato's and Dante's. Both agree on three points: (a) the experience is a genuine revelation, not a delusion; (b) the erotic mode of the vision prefigures a kind of love in which the sexual element is transformed and transcended; (c) he who has once seen the glory of the Uncreated revealed indirectly in the glory of a creature can henceforth never be fully satisfied with anything less than a direct encounter with the former. About everything else they disagree radically.   (F&A 65)

In delineating these differences Auden focuses chiefly on what he believes to be Plato's inadequate notion of the human person; but he also points out that their understanding of the *scala amoris* is very different: "The Vision of Eros is not, according to Dante, the first rung of a long ladder: there is only one step to take, from the personal creature who can love and be loved to the personal Creator who is Love" (68).

11. The title of Auden's *Nation* review of *Love in the Western World* is "Agape and Eros," which may not mean anything, but in any event Nygren's is not the sort of book Auden would have missed. A fairly substantial comment on it comes in a book Auden knew very well, Reinhold Niebuhr's *The Nature and Destiny of Man*: though Niebuhr calls *Agape and Eros* "profound," he also chastises Nygren

for attempting to enforce his distinctions too rigorously: "It is significant that Jesus does not regard the contrast between natural human love and the divine *agape* as absolute," he says, then quotes Matthew 7:11—"If ye then, being evil, know how to give good gifts unto your children, how much more shall your Father which is in heaven give good things to them that ask him"—in support of his claim (II:84n).

12. From an essay in *Theology* (November 1950), quoted by Carpenter (300).

13. This is perhaps as good a place as any to quote, as I feel I must, Randall Jarrell's unjust but stimulating and hilarious description of the later Auden on love: "Eros, considered as the not-yet-mutated Agape into which Agape is continually relapsing, has gained a new respectability: it is Grandmother, who was not everything she might have been, but who left us all the money for the Asylum. Sexuality is now no more than a relatively minor aspect of our religious life. Auden explains, in a summary of Kierkegaard, that for the individual once exposed to Christianity—whether or not he believes—there are only three possibilities: marriage, celibacy, or despair.... I'm not sure which of these possibilities Auden thinks of as his own state; probably he, as usual, considers all three 'aspects of one Reality,' and thus can credit himself with one-third of each" ("Freud" 178–79).

14. Edward Mendelson here, as so often, has a properly nuanced view of the matter: "Auden never approved of his sexuality, but he learned to acknowledge that it was not a uniquely isolating tribulation that barred him forever from the community of love. He came to recognize it instead as one of the infinitely varied forms of crookedness whose name, in his later work, was sin—and which was therefore open to forgiveness" (*Early* 237). Mendelson echoes Auden's own language, not only the "If sins can be forgiven" of "In Praise of Limestone," but also the complex word "crookedness," which turns up several times in Auden's early work, most notably in "As I Walked Out One Evening" (" 'You shall love your crooked neighbour / With your crooked heart' " [CP 135]) and "The chimneys are smoking" ("And since our desire cannot take that route which is straightest, / Let us choose the crooked" [EA 118]).

15. The roots of Auden's thinking on this question lie in a passage from Kierkegaard's *Journals*, and interestingly enough, Kierkagaard takes the position of "Dichtung und Wahrheit": to the person who claims to have been liberated from sin by Christ, "the only conceivable objection would be: but you might possibly have been saved in a different way. To that he cannot answer. It is as though one were to say to someone in love, yes, but you might have fallen in love with another girl: to which he would have to answer: there is no answer to that, for I only know that she is my love. The moment a lover can answer that objection he is *eo ipso* not in love. If a believer can answer that objection he is *eo ipso* not a believer" (#922).

16. In the second volume of Art Spiegelman's comic-book-style history of his father's experiences during the Holocaust, *Maus II*, Spiegelman's therapist (a Holocaust survivor himself) says "maybe it's better not to have any more stories." To which Spiegelman: "Uh-huh. Samuel Beckett once said: 'Every word is like an unnecessary stain on silence and nothingness.'" Therapist: "Uh-huh." Silence. Then Spiegelman: "On the other hand, he SAID it" (45).

17. Carpenter has rightly spoken of "the dry, almost agnostic character of Auden's faith," and quotes from a sermon Auden once preached to illustrate the point (298). In many of his letters, especially a few he wrote late in life to his Oxford tutor Nevill Coghill (in the Berg Collection), he can sound agnostic indeed. But given his repetitive insistence that "orthodoxy is reticence"—see the last sentence of this paragraph—it is not clear what to make of this agnostic tone. According to Ursula Niebuhr, to whom he may have spoken more freely and frequently about religious matters than to anyone else, he once said of the Resurrection: "It does make a difference if it really happened, doesn't it?" (Spender, *Tribute* 108)

18. An incomplete listing of the places where Auden uses the phrase "orthodoxy is reticence," which he attributed to an Anglican bishop he never named: *The Viking Book of Aphorisms*, F&A 71, DH 21, and, in question form, in the last lines of "'The Truest Poetry is the Most Feigning,'" cited as the epigraph to this chapter. (Note that this poem suggests that one should be reticent about all forms of love.) Incidentally—given the later Auden's frequently expressed claim that, had he taken holy orders, he would eventually have become a bishop—Edward Mendelson suspects that the Auden himself is the author of the statement.

Very similar is the claim, in "Ode to Terminus," that "to all species except the talkative / have been allotted the niche and diet that / become them" (CP 810). And an analogous admonishment of the talkative comes in Schoenberg's opera *Moses und Aron*, in which Aaron's florid tenor is countered by Moses's stolid speech, his refusal to sing. "It is true," writes Daniel Albright, "that Moses is permitted once in the opera to sing; but what he sings—'Purify your thinking. Free it from worthless things. Consecrate it with truth"—could be paraphrased to mean, in context, Shut up" (*Representation* 38).

CHAPTER 6: ARIEL AND THE MENIPPEA

1. As Seamus Heaney has pointed out (110), a relatively early and wonderfully vivid formulation of this contrast comes in Auden's 1937 poem "Orpheus":

> What does the song hope for? And his moved hands
> A little way from the birds, the shy, the delightful?
>   To be bewildered and happy,
>   Or most of all the knowledge of life? (CP 158)

If Ariel poets are content to be "bewildered and happy," the Prosperos among us will seek "the knowledge of life."

2. "Group's handful of Sunday nighters were scarcely the masses: 'small Sabbatical assemblies' of bourgeois Lefties in 'juvenile beards, dark-blue shirts, and horn-rimmed spectacles, which are not the representative insignia of the working class', was how Ivor Brown saw them. . . . Brown couldn't 'see much point' in audiences who 'either see the point of the propaganda already or see the point of nothing but their own importance'" (Cunningham 323). Brown's comments appeared in his essay "Left Theatres," in *The New Statesman*, 6 April 1935.

3. However, Michael Sidnell cites several Marxist reviewers and commentators who suspected not only the play's political effectiveness but also Auden's intentions (68–70).

4. In one sense, of course, Auden's interest in the carnivalesque goes back to the beginning of his career, though perhaps he would not have known the term then. One of his earliest works, *Paid on Both Sides* (significantly subtitled "A Charade"), uses characters from the old "mummer's play" or "Play of St. George," typically associated with Christmas carnivals. (Given Auden's early love of Hardy, one wonders if he had read and taken note of the key scene in *The Return of the Native*, where Eustacia Vye substitutes for one of the actors in the mummer's play in order to meet Clym Yeobright.) *The Dance of Death* is modeled, of course, on the peculiar medieval genre of the *danse macabre*, a kind of carnivalized tragedy; Auden had given a *danse macabre* poem to Rupert Brooke, who then commissioned Auden to write his own modern version (Mendelson 268, Sidnell 66). And when *The Dance of Death* was performed at the Westminster Theatre (in private performance, on two Sundays in 1934), it was paired with a mystery play, *The Deluge*, from the Chester cycle. So these roots go very deep for Auden.

When the Group Theatre revived *The Dance of Death* in 1935, it was paired with a rather different play: Eliot's *Sweeney Agonistes*. One of the interesting minor themes that emerges from Sidnell's excellent book is Eliot's changing reaction to Auden's dramatic work. He thought *Paid on Both Sides* "a brilliant piece of work" and eagerly published it in *The Criterion* (Sidnell 64); and when he saw *The Dance of Death* he liked it very much—at first. His later comments, on this and on the Auden-Isherwood plays, were much more critical (e.g., 94, 202). I attribute this change to Eliot's move (noted earlier in this chapter) away from mixed genres and popular genres and towards what Bakhtin might call more monological genres or drama.

For a fuller account of Auden, Eliot, and modern English drama, see my forthcoming essay, "Auden and the Dream of Public Poetry," in *Literature and the Renewal of the Public Sphere*, ed. Susan VanZanten Gallagher and Mark Walhout (London: Macmillan; New York: St. Martin's).

5. Auden spent his last two years at Gresham's School "in the exclusive study of chemistry, zoology, and botany" (F&A 498), and went up to Oxford as a science student, only shifting to English in the middle of his first year.

APPENDIX: AUDEN AND MERTON AT THE MOVIES

1. In a recent essay in the *New Yorker*, Nicholas Jenkins describes the film as a "newsreel" that accompanied the showing of a German comedy (96). It is not clear whether this account is at variance with those of Carpenter and Davenport-Hines.

2. Fifteen years earlier, though, Auden had written about his return to the Church without mentioning the episode in Yorkville. At that time, another experience, one from the Spanish Civil War, was on his mind: "On arriving in Barcelona, I found as I walked through the city that all the churches were closed and there was not a priest to be seen. To my astonishment, this discovery left me profoundly shocked and disturbed. . . . I could not escape acknowledging that, however I had consciously ignored and rejected the Church for sixteen years, the existence of churches and what went on in them had all the time been very important to me. If that was the case, what then?" (*Modern* 41)

3. On Auden's political disillusionment and its poetic consequences, the best analysis remains Mendelson's (*Early Auden* 196–200, 314–23).

4. On the history of this poem, see Carpenter 330–31, 415, 418. Davenport-Hines attributes Auden's dislike of the poem to Lyndon Johnson's use (and misquotation) of the "we must love one another or die" line in a television ad used in the 1964 presidential campaign (319), but the poem disappeared from collections gathered by Auden some years earlier.

5. It is worth noting that Merton, like Auden, was an ambiguous citizen. His mother was American, but his father was from New Zealand. He was born in France and, though he grew up mostly on Long Island, got a good deal of his education in England (including some time at Cambridge University). Merton certainly never thought of himself as an American in any conventional sense, nor could he have done so.

Works Cited

Abrams, M. H. *Natural Supernaturalism: Tradition and Revolution in English Literature*. New York: Norton, 1971.

Albright, Daniel. *Lyricality in English Literature*. Lincoln: U of Nebraska P, 1985.

———. *Representation and the Imagination: Beckett, Kafka, Nabokov, Schoenberg*. Chicago: U of Chicago P, 1981.

Alighieri, Dante. *La Vita Nuova*. Trans. Barbara Reynolds. Harmondsworth: Penguin, 1969.

Althaus, Paul. *The Theology of Martin Luther*. Trans. Robert C. Shultz. Philadelphia: Fortress Press, 1966.

Abrams, M. H. *The Mirror and the Lamp*. New York: Oxford UP, 1953.

Ansen, Alan. *The Table Talk of W. H. Auden*. Ed. Nicholas Jenkins. London: Faber, 1990.

Auden, W. H. *A Certain World: A Commonplace Book*. London: Faber, 1970.

———. *Collected Poems*. Ed. Edward Mendelson. Rev. ed. London: Faber, 1991.

———. "Criticism in a Mass Society." *The Intent of the Critic*. Ed. Donald A. Stauffer. Princeton: Princeton UP, 1941. 127–47.

———. *The Double Man*. New York: Random, 1941.

———. *The Dyer's Hand*. New York: Random, 1962.

———. *The Enchafèd Flood*. 1950. Charlottesville: U of Virginia P, 1979.

———. *The English Auden*. Ed. Edward Mendelson. London: Faber, 1977.

———. "Eros and Agape." *Nation* 152. 26 (28 June 1941). 756–58.

———. *Forewords and Afterwords*. New York: Random, 1973.

———. *Juvenilia: Poems, 1922–1928*. Ed. Katherine Bucknell. Princeton: Princeton UP, 1994.

———. "The Means of Grace." *New Republic* 104.1383 (2 June 1941). 765–66.

———. "Pope." *From Anne to Victoria: Essays by Various Hands*. Ed. Bonamy Dobrée. New York: Scribner, 1937. 89–107.

———. "A Preface to Kierkegaard." *New Republic* 110.1537 (15 May 1944). 683–86.

————. *The Prolific and the Devourer*. New York: Ecco, 1976, 1981.

————. *Secondary Worlds*. London: Faber, 1968.

————. *Selected Poems*. Ed. Edward Mendelson. New ed. New York: Vintage, 1979.

————. *Selected Poetry*. New York: Modern Library, 1958.

————. "Squares and Oblongs." *Poets at Work*. Ed. Charles A. Abbott. New York: Harcourt, 1948. 163–81.

————. Untitled essay. *Modern Canterbury Pilgrims*. Ed. James A. Pike. London: Mowbray, 1956.

————. Untitled essay. *Religion and the Intellectuals*. PR Series 3. New York: Partisan Review, 1950.

————. *W. H. Auden and Chester Kallman: Libretti and Other Dramatic Writings by W. H. Auden, 1939–1973*. Ed. Edward Mendelson. Princeton: Princeton UP, 1993. Vol. 2 of *The Complete Works of W. H. Auden*.

————. *W. H. Auden and Christopher Isherwood: Plays, and Other Dramatic Writings by W. H. Auden, 1928–1938*. Ed. Edward Mendelson. Princeton: Princeton UP, 1988. Vol. 1 of *The Complete Works of W. H. Auden*.

Auden, W. H., and Norman Holmes Pearson, eds. *Poets of the English Language, Volume V*. New York: Viking, 1950.

Auden, W. H., and Louis MacNeice. *Letters from Iceland*. 1937. London: Faber, 1965.

Bakhtin, Mikhail. *The Dialogic Imagination*. Trans. Caryl Emerson and Michael Holquist. Austin: U of Texas P, 1981.

————. *Problems of Dostoevsky's Poetics*. Ed. and Trans. Caryl Emerson. Minneapolis: U of Minnesota P, 1984.

Baudelaire, Charles. *Les Fleurs du Mal*. Trans. Richard Howard. Boston: Godine, 1982.

Berg Collection of English and American Literature at The New York Public Library (Astor, Lenox and Tilden Foundations).

Berry, Wendell. "Does Community Have A Value?" *Home Economics*. San Francisco: North Point, 1987. 179–92.

Blair, John G. *The Poetic Art of W. H. Auden*. Princeton: Princeton UP, 1965.

Blake, William. *Complete Poetry and Prose*. Ed. David V. Erdman. Rev. ed. Garden City: Anchor, 1982.

Boswell, James. *Life of Johnson*. Ed. R. W. Chapman. Oxford: Oxford UP, 1980.

Brodsky, Joseph. *Less Than One: Selected Essays*. New York: Farrar, 1986.

Bucknell, Katherine, and Nicholas Jenkins, eds. *"In Solitude, for Company": W. H. Auden After 1940: Unpublished Prose and Recent Criticism*. Auden Studies 3. Oxford: Clarendon, 1995.

————. *W. H. Auden: "The Language of Learning and the Language of Love":*
Uncollected Writings; New Interpretations. Auden Studies 2. Oxford:
Clarendon, 1994.

————. *W. H. Auden: "The Map of All My Youth": Early Works, Friends, and*
Influences. Auden Studies 1. Oxford: Clarendon, 1990.

Bush, Ronald. *T. S. Eliot: A Study in Character and Style.* New York: Oxford
UP, 1984.

Callan, Edward. *Auden: A Carnival of Intellect.* New York: Oxford UP, 1983.

Camus, Albert. *Resistance, Rebellion, and Death.* Trans. Justin O'Brien. New
York: Vintage, 1974.

Carpenter, Humphrey. *W. H. Auden: A Biography.* Boston: Houghton Mifflin,
1981.

Cavaliero, Glen. *Charles Williams: Poet of Theology.* Grand Rapids: Eerdmans,
1983.

Cunningham, Valentine. *British Writers of the Thirties.* Oxford: Oxford UP, 1989.

Davenport-Hines, Richard. *Auden.* New York: Pantheon, 1995.

Deedy, John. *Auden as Didymus: the Poet as Columnist Anonymous.* Mt. Vernon,
N.Y.: Appel, 1993.

Duchêne, François. *The Case of The Helmeted Airman: A Study of W. H.*
Auden's Poetry. London: Chatto, 1972.

Eliot, T. S. *Collected Poems: 1909–1962.* New York: Harcourt, 1963.

————. *On Poetry and Poets.* New York: Farrar, 1957.

————. *The Sacred Wood.* London: Methuen, 1920.

————. *Selected Essays.* New York: Harcourt, 1950.

Farnan, Dorothy J. *Auden in Love.* New York: Simon & Schuster, 1984.

Fish, Stanley. *Doing What Comes Naturally.* Durham: Duke UP, 1989.

————. *There's No Such Thing as Free Speech and It's a Good Thing, Too.* New
York: Oxford UP, 1994.

Foucault, Michel. *Discipline and Punish: the Birth of the Prison.* Trans. Alan
Sheridan. New York: Pantheon, 1977.

————. *The Order of Things: An Archaeology of the Human Sciences.* [translator
not identified] New York: Random, 1970.

Frye, Northrop. *Anatomy of Criticism: Four Essays.* Princeton: Princeton UP,
1957.

Fuller, John. *A Reader's Guide to W. H. Auden.* New York: Farrar, 1970.

Fussell, Paul. "Modernism, Adversary Culture, and Edmund Blunden."
Thank God for the Atom Bomb and Other Essays. New York: Ballantine,
1988. 211–32.

Gadamer, Hans-Georg. *Truth and Method.* 2nd. ed. Trans. revised by Joel
Weinsheimer and Donald G. Marshall. New York: Crossroad, 1992.

Goethe, Johann Wolfgang. *Italian Journey*. Trans. W. H. Auden and Elizabeth Mayer. Harmondsworth: Penguin, 1962.

Graff, Gerald. *Literature Against Itself*. Chicago: U of Chicago P, 1979.

Gramsci, Antonio. *Selections from the Prison Notebooks*. Ed. and Trans. Quentin Hoare and Geoffrey Nowell Smith. New York: International, 1971.

Habermas, Jürgen. *The Philosophical Discourse of Modernity*. Trans. Frederick Lawrence. Cambridge: MIT, 1990.

———. *The Theory of Communicative Action*. Trans. Thomas McCarthy. 2 vols. Boston: Beacon, 1985, 1989.

Heaney, Seamus. *The Government of the Tongue*. London: Faber, 1988.

Hecht, Anthony. *The Hidden Law: The Poetry of W. H. Auden*. Cambridge: Harvard UP, 1993.

Horace. *The Complete Odes and Epodes*. Trans. W. G. Shepherd. Harmondsworth: Penguin, 1983.

———. *Satires and Epistles*. Trans. Smith Palmer Bovie. Chicago: U of Chicago P, 1959.

Hynes, Samuel. *The Auden Generation: Literature and Politics in England in the 1930s*. Princeton: Princeton UP, 1972.

———. "The Voice of Exile: Auden in 1940." *Sewanee Review* 90.1 (winter 1982): 31–52.

Isherwood, Christopher. *Christopher and His Kind*. New York: Farrar, 1976.

Jacobs, Alan. "The Unnatural Practices of Stanley Fish." *South Atlantic Review* 55.4 (November 1990): 87–98.

Jarrell, Randall. "Freud to Paul: the Stages of Auden's Ideology." *The Third Book of Criticism*. New York: Farrar, 1969. 153–90.

———. *Kipling, Auden & Company: Essays and Reviews 1935–1964*. New York: Farrar, 1980.

Jenkins, Nicholas. "Goodbye 1939: How New York Gave Birth to the Auden Revival." *New Yorker* 1 April 1996: 88–97.

Johnson, Samuel. *Lives of the English Poets*. 3 vols. Oxford: Clarendon, 1905. Ed. George Birkbeck Hill. New York: Octagon, 1967.

Kermode, Frank. *Romantic Image*. New York: Macmillan, 1957.

Kierkegaard, Soren. *Either/Or*. Trans. Alastair Hannay. Harmondsworth: Penguin, 1992.

———. *Journals*. Trans. and Ed. Alexander Dru. New York: Oxford UP, 1938.

Langbaum, Robert. *The Poetry of Experience*. 1957. New York: Norton, 1963.

Larkin, Philip. "What's Become of Wystan?" *Required Writing: Miscellaneous Pieces, 1955–1982*. New York: Farrar, 1982. 123–28.

Lasch, Christopher. "The Communitarian Critique of Liberalism." *Soundings* 69.1 (spring/summer 1986): 60–75.

Levy, Alan. "On Audenstrasse: In the Autumn of the Age of Anxiety." *New York Times Magazine* 8 August 1971: 10+.

Lottman, Herbert R. *Albert Camus: A Biography*. Garden City, N.Y.: Doubleday, 1979.

MacIntyre, Alasdair. "Traditions and Conflicts." *Liberal Education* 73.5 (November/December 1987): 6–13.

——. *Whose Justice? Which Rationality?* Notre Dame: U of Notre Dame P, 1988.

Mack, Maynard. *Alexander Pope: a Life*. New York: Norton, 1985.

Mannheim, Karl. *Ideology and Utopia*. Trans. Louis Wirth and Edward Shils. New York: Harcourt, 1953.

McDiarmid, Lucy. *Auden's Apologies for Poetry*. Princeton: Princeton UP, 1990.

——. *Saving Civilization: Yeats, Eliot, and Auden Between the Wars*. Cambridge: Cambridge UP, 1984.

McGann, Jerome J. *The Romantic Ideology: A Critical Investigation*. Chicago: U of Chicago P, 1983.

Meilaender, Gilbert. *Friendship: A Study in Theological Ethics*. Notre Dame: U of Notre Dame P, 1981.

Mendelson, Edward. *Early Auden*. 1981. Cambridge: Harvard UP, 1983.

Merton, Thomas. *The Secular Journal*. New York: Farrar, 1959.

——. *The Seven Storey Mountain*. New York: Harcourt, 1948.

Miller, J. Hillis. *The Disappearance of God*. 1963. Cambridge: Harvard UP, 1965.

Milosz, Czeslaw. *The Witness of Poetry*. Cambridge: Harvard UP, 1983.

Mott, Michael. *The Seven Mountains of Thomas Merton*. Boston: Houghton, 1984.

Murdoch, Iris. *Metaphysics as a Guide to Morals*. 1992. Harmondsworth: Penguin, 1993.

Niebuhr, Reinhold. *The Nature and Destiny of Man*. 2 vols. New York: Scribner, 1943.

Nygren, Anders. *Agape and Eros*. Trans. Philip S. Watson. London: SPCK, 1953.

O'Loughlin, Michael. *The Garlands of Repose*. Chicago: U of Chicago P, 1979.

Pascal, Blaise. *Pensées*. Trans. A. J. Krailsheimer. Harmondsworth: Penguin, 1966.

Pope, Alexander. *The Poems of Alexander Pope*. Ed. John Butt. New Haven: Yale UP, 1963.

Repogle, Justin. *Auden's Poetry*. Seattle: U of Washington P, 1969.

Ricks, Christopher. *T. S. Eliot and Prejudice*. London: Faber, 1988.

Ricoeur, Paul. *Freud and Philosophy*. Trans. Denis Savage. New Haven: Yale UP, 1970.

Rudd, Niall. Introduction. *The Satires*. By Juvenal. Trans. Niall Rudd. Oxford: Oxford UP, 1991.

Scott, Nathan A., Jr. *The Poetry of Civic Virtue*. Philadelphia: Fortress, 1976.

Sidnell, Michael J. *Dances of Death: the Group Theatre of London in the Thirties*. London: Faber, 1984.

Smith, Stan. *W.H. Auden*. New York: Blackwell, 1985.

Spears, Monroe K. *The Poetry of W. H. Auden: the Disenchanted Island*. New York: Oxford UP, 1963.

Spence, Jonathan D. *The Memory Palace of Matteo Ricci*. New York: Viking, 198.

Spender, Stephen. *World Within World*. New York: Harcourt, 1951.

———, ed. *W. H. Auden: A Tribute*. New York: Macmillan, 1975.

Spiegelman, Art. *Maus: A Survivor's Tale, II: And Now My Troubles Began*. New York: Pantheon, 1991.

Taylor, Charles. *Sources of the Self: the Making of the Modern Identity*. Cambridge: Harvard UP, 1989.

Walzer, Michael. *The Company of Critics: Social Criticism and Political Commitment in the Twentieth Century*. New York: Basic, 1988.

Weil, Simone. *Waiting for God*. Trans. Emma Craufurd. New York: Harper, 1951.

Weinbrot, Howard D. *Eighteenth-Century Satire: Essays on Texts and Contexts*. Cambridge: Cambridge UP, 1988.

Williams, Charles. *The Descent of the Dove*. 1939. Grand Rapids: Eerdmans, 1980.

Williams, Raymond. *The Country and the City*. New York: Oxford UP, 1973.

Woods, Gregory. *Articulate Flesh: Male Homoeroticism and Modern Poetry*. New Haven: Yale UP, 1988.

Yeats, W. B. *Collected Poems of W. B. Yeats*. Ed. Richard Finneran. New York: Macmillan, 1983, 1989.

———. *Essays and Introductions*. New York: Macmillan, 1961.

Index

New Jerusalem. *See* Arcadians and
 Utopians
Niebuhr, Reinhold, 5, 6, 87, 142n, 146n
Niebuhr, Ursula, 148n
Nietzsche, Friedrich, 10
Nygren, Anders, 83, 146n

occasional verse, 26
opera, 91–94, 101–2, 105

Pascal, Blaise, 13, 88, 134n
Peele, George, 100
Pelagius, 117
Pindar, 42
Plato, 10, 56, 82, 146n
Pope, Alexander, 34–40, 101, 143n
Pound, Ezra, 131
psychoanalysis, 10–11, 13, 113, 119

Quennell, Peter, 38

Rabelais, François, 141
Repogle, Justin, 136n
Ricci, Matteo, 68
Ricoeur, Paul, 24
Riefensthal, Leni, 121
romanticism, chapter 2 passim, 135–36n
Rorty, Richard, 5, 7, 9, 134n

Schlegel, August Wilhelm, 135n
Schoenberg, Arnold, 148n
science, 110–11
Scott, Nathan A., Jr., 25
self, selfhood, 4–5, 20–22
Shakespeare, William, 16, 113, 127
Shelley, Percy Bysshe, 15, 22, 27, 119,
 127, 135n, 136n
Sidnell, Michael, 113, 114
Silone, Ignazio, 9

Smith, Stan, xv, 118, 134n
Smith, Sydney, 43, 61
Spain, and Spanish Civil War, 59, 125
Spears, Monroe, xiv, xv, 97, 133n
Spence, Jonathan, 68
Spender, Stephen, 86, 87, 98, 133n, 138n,
 142n
Spiegelman, Art, 148n
Stalin, Joseph, 47, 61
Strauss, Richard, 139n
Stravinsky, Igor, xv, 134n, 139n

Taylor, Charles, 4
Taylor, Jeremy, 57
Tillich, Paul, 136n
Tolkien, J. R. R., 37, 139n
Tollner, Ernst, 26
Tradition, and traditions, xvii–xviii, 8–10,
 12, 31, 35, 65–66, 76, afterword passim

Utopians. *See* Arcadians and Utopians

Verdi, Giuseppe, 102
Versailles, Treaty of, 122, 125
Virgil, 57, 109–10, 112, 141n
Voltaire, 137n

Wagner, Richard, 91, 93
Weil, Simone, 68, 72
Williams, Charles, 25, 26, 37, 82–83, 84,
 139n, 142–43n
Williams, Raymond, 136n
Wodehouse, P. G., 113
Woods, Gregory, 78, 81
Wordsworth, William, 21, 22, 27, 105,
 135n, 136n

Yeats, William Butler, xiv, 21, 24, 26, 34,
 35, 53, 90, 116, 131, 138–39n